The Genius Famine

Why we need geniuses,
Why they're dying out,
and
Why we must rescue them

The Genius Famine

Why we need geniuses,
Why they're dying out,
and
Why we must rescue them

Edward Dutton
and
Bruce G Charlton

The University of Buckingham Press

First published in Great Britain in 2015 by

The University of Buckingham Press
Yeomanry House
Hunter Street
Buckingham MK18 1EG

© The University of Buckingham Press

ISBN 9781908684608

Printed and bound in Great Britain by
Marston Book Services Ltd, Oxfordshire

Acknowledgements – Both authors acknowledge the influence of Dr. Michael A. Woodley, both in general terms and also in relation to several specific aspects of the argument of this book; although we take full responsibility for the use we have made of these ideas. In addition, Edward Dutton would like to thank Dr. Dimitri van der Linden for assorted stimulating conversations on the topics in this book. He would also like to thank his wife, Mimmi, and children Martha and Henry. Bruce Charlton wishes to acknowledge the essential support and encouragement of his wife, Gill; and his children, Billy and Nancy.

Contents

Introduction

This book is about genius: what it is, what it does, where it comes from.[1]

And about geniuses: especially why there used to be so many and now there are so few; what was the effect of an era of geniuses, and what will be the consequences of our current Genius Famine.

This book describes the genius as an Endogenous personality; that is, a person of high intelligence combined with a personality driven from within, an 'inner' –orientated personality: that is, a dominated by the Creative Triad of (1) Innate high ability, (2) Inner motivation and (3) Intuitive thinking.

When high intelligence and this type of personality are confluent, a potential genius is the result. But to fulfil this potential the Endogenous personality must find and accept his own Destiny, and must undergo the trials and tribulations of a Quest before he is likely to be rewarded by an Illumination: a breakthrough.

Even then, the breakthrough must be noticed, understood, accepted, implemented by society at

---

[1] This book is mostly derived from Bruce Charlton's blog: *Intelligence, Personality and Genius* http://iqpersonalitygenius.blogspot.co.uk

large; and we describe how past societies were much better at recognizing and making a place for the potential genius. Because the problem is that the Endogenous personality is usually an awkward and asocial character at best; and often an actively unpleasant person and a disruptive influence.

Geniuses are altruistic, in the sense that their work is primarily for the good of the group; and not for the usual social rewards such as status, money, sex, and popularity.

Therefore many geniuses need to be sustained in a long-term way; and their work demands careful attention and evaluation.

We argue that modern societies, by means both indirect and direct, have become hostile to genius and indifferent to the work of those relatively few remaining geniuses.

However, because the work of a genius is necessary and irreplaceable, we argue for a change of attitude. Modern society needs geniuses for its own survival in the face of unfamiliar, often unprecedented, threats. Therefore, we must in future do a better job of recognizing, sustaining and accepting guidance from as many geniuses of the highest quality that can be found.

Chapter One

What is the Endogenous Personality?

What is the Endogenous Personality? And why is he so important?

In a nutshell, we argue that the Endogenous personality is the type of a potential genius – a compound of abilities and attitudes, of intelligence and innerness. As a strong generalization: the true geniuses are Endogenous personalities; and it is from Endogenous personalities that geniuses arise.

The Endogenous personality is the 'inner' Man; a person whose outlook on life is 'inward.' He is inner-directed, inner-driven, inner-motivated; one who uses inner modes of thinking, inner evaluations, in-tuition; one who is to a high degree autonomous, self-sufficient; one who is relatively indifferent to social pressures, influences and inducements.

He stands in stark contrast to the Exogenous personality; that is, to most people. The Exogenous Personality is orientated toward the environment, particularly the social environment. These are people who want more than anything else social (including sexual) status, worldly success; people whose perceptions are directed outwards and who try to align their behaviour with group norms.

When described in such terms, the Endogenous personality might appear anti-social, uncooperative, a dreamer, not the kind of person we might wish to have to deal with on a regular basis. We would probably be accurate in perceiving the Endogenous Personality in this negative way. We probably wouldn't want to go for a drink with him, let alone be friends with him.

But he is important; he is very important. Because the Endogenous personality is the archetypal 'genius.' He is the *type* of a genius – whether a large scale, world historical genius of the highest level achieved by humanity – a Shakespeare, a Beethoven or an Einstein – or a local, tribal, or town genius; a shaman, a sculptor, an inventor whose name is unrecorded (yet who might be the originator of some great but anonymous ballad, folk song, painting – or a technological breakthrough such as the spade, spear-thrower, arch or stirrup).

Genuine 'breakthrough', world-impact creativity is so rare, so difficult (far more difficult than commonly imagined) that it requires a special kind of mind – a mind especially designed for this kind of work (inner work). There need not be many such men – indeed, there should not be too many, since the necessary mind is relatively unfit for the primary, day-to-day, activities of survival and reproduction of the species. But such men are needed – sooner or later, from time to time.

These are the people who (whether we know their names or not) will almost-certainly be behind the scientific and technical breakthroughs that are the motor of civilization, these are people whose can inspire and unite society moving it towards greater things or out of the depths of despair and *ennui*; these are the people who can rescue a society on the brink of catastrophe.

The Endogenous personality is recognized because when this kind of creative personality is combined with high 'general intelligence', we get a potential genius – of greatness in proportion to their ability.

So, an Inner, Intuitive personality plus high Intelligence (or another special ability) is the Creative Triad and equals the Endogenous personality, or potential genius. The high intelligence serves as a kind of guarantee that the Endogenous personality is *positively adapted* by his lop-sided focus, and inclination to be a creative specialist problem-solver in society; and is not merely a broken, sick or damaged individual who simply *cannot* participate in normal society – perhaps through mental or physical illness.

The Endogenous personality will stay focused on a problem longer than most men – and he will look at the problem in a different way. He will deploy different (more inward) procedures of understanding – more detached, more abstracting. Hence he is more likely to see something new and useful in a new and different way.

His stance is less personal. He stands back to a greater extent than most. He sees the problem in a wider scope precisely because he sees the problem detached from normal personal concerns, such as status, sex, or wealth; none of which he really seems to care much about. For him, solving his problem is not a means to an end – a way of gaining status, wealth or sex – it is an end in itself. The inner man gets the greatest satisfaction from inner work – it is what he most wants to do.

In this short book, we will explore the Genius; the Endogenous type of personality including its exceptionally high intelligence. We will argue that the highly able Endogenous personality is indeed the archetypal genius; the engine, in particular, of the original innovations that are vital to civilization itself. Without genius, civilization will certainly continue to decline (and we will show that it *is* declining), and eventually collapse. With more geniuses, taken notice of, the process would be slowed and – who knows? – perhaps some genius could discover a way out?

We will demonstrate, in more depth, the importance to any society of nurturing a small number of such personalities; and, worryingly, we will find

4

that they are less likely to manifest themselves now than was the case just a few generations ago.

We will argue, indeed, that we have a Genius Famine. Genius has now all-but disappeared from public view; partly because intelligence (which is strongly genetic) is in decline in the West, partly because social institutions no longer recognize or nurture genius, and partly because the modern West is actively hostile to genius.

Finally, we will look at what – if anything – can be done to rescue the genius and thus preserve civilization.

However, in order to understand the Endogenous Personality, we need to understand the nature of personality itself, as well as the nature of intelligence, as these two traits are at the heart of the Endogenous personality and of Genius.

Chapter Two

What is Personality, What is Intelligence?

Intelligence and Personality are the two main ways that psychologists have developed for describing differences between people.

In brief – Intelligence is an ability, while personality is character; intelligence is general – with the level of intelligence affecting many specific abilities, while personality can be understood as a pattern of motivations, preferences, satisfactions.

In terms of computers – intelligence is something like the processing speed, while personality is about the types of software installed. Or, intelligence is about the efficiency of the brain, while personality is about what that brain is designed to do. Or intelligence is about how well the brain works; while personality describes the circuitry, the hard-wiring – what *kind* of brain it is.

A further difference is that intelligence is measured by tests – IQ tests; while personality is evaluated by human beings – either self-rated using self-describing scales, or else rated by other people.

But a similarity is that both IQ and personality are (nearly always) comparative measurements. A person high in intelligence, or high on a personality trait such as Conscientiousness, is 'high' *relative to other people*. 'High' or 'Low', in both intelligence and personality, therefore does *not* describe an objective measurement of a personal attribute in the way that (for example) high or low blood pressure or blood sugar measurements would.

Personality

Personality is, in essence, our general way of being. Differences in personality predict differences in how people will respond in a certain situation.

Personality evaluations are usually measured by questionnaires: How close to you does a car moving at a certain speed have to be before you judge that it is too dangerous to cross the road in front of it? How many annoying things have to happen to you in a day before you lose your temper and raise your voice? How strongly do the emotions of others impact how you feel?

Different people will give different answers to these questions, in part because of variation in their personality. Typically, people are asked whether a certain behaviour, or like or dislike, is present or absent in them; or else asked to rate its strength. Multiple such questions can be analysed and averaged to yield a few personality 'traits' which cluster together.

8

The exact number of these traits used by psychologists depends on the purpose of the personality evaluation. The number can be as few as one general master trait (e.g. pro-social *versus* asocial – see below), or dozens of specific traits such as aggression, or courage – but usually, for convenience, the number of traits used for describing personality have been something between about two and five.

Although we will be suggesting revisions and improvements to the scheme, many psychologists currently suggest that personality can best be understood in terms of five essential personality characteristics: these are the 'Big 5', which each make a scale between extremes separated by a dash:

(1) *Extraversion–Introversion*. Extraversion is a need for external stimulation – especially social stimulation; introversion is sufficient internal stimulation therefore independence from external stimuli.

(2) *Neuroticism–Emotional Stability*.
Neuroticism relates to emotional instability – especially negative mood swings such as anxiety, depression, shyness.

(3) *Conscientiousness–Impulsiveness*:
Conscientiousness refers to responsivity to social norms, usually leading to organized and self-disciplined behaviour.

(4) *Agreeableness* (which is essentially the same as the Empathizing trait)–Indifference to other people: Agreeableness shows itself in a high interest in other people, what they are thinking and how they feel.

(5) *Openness-Intellect–Aversion to change/ intellectual conservatism*: Openness references intellectual curiosity and a preference for novelty, creativity (in some sense of the word), hypnotisability, unusual psychological experiences. Openness weakly but significantly correlates with intelligence, as it is measuring some of the same things.

These five personality traits are (except for Openness–Intellect) regarded as independent of IQ scores (at least within normal IQ ranges); and our placing on them predicts how we behave.

For example, high Conscientiousness as a child predicts greater success in education and employment; high Neuroticism predicts problems with mood swings, anxiety and depression. High Openness-Intellect will tend to result in being a novelty-loving, impractical, perhaps artistic, academic or spiritual dreamer. A moderately high score, however, is a predictor of artistic success – or at least, on some measures of artistic success that focus on the production of novelty (although, we will argue, High Openness does not predict the genius type of creativity).[2]

The Big Five were developed from the Big Three traits defined by psychologist Hans J. Eysenck (1916-1997), who arrived in England from Germany in the 1930s and became the most dominant personality in British academic psychology. The Big Three are Extraversion, Neuroticism and Psychoticism.[3] In effect, the Big Five dimensions of Conscientiousness and Agree-ableness are the opposites of various aspects of Eysenck's Psychoticism; and Openness takes some aspects of Psychoticism and blends them with behaviours characteristic of modern intellectuals (as may be inferred from this description, we regard the Openness trait as a concept of dubious biological validity).

Like Eysenck, the British-born Canadian psychologist J. Philippe Rushton (1943-2012) was an original thinker, unafraid to tackle controversial

---

[2] For a more detailed introduction to 'personality' see Nettle, D. (2007). *Personality: What Makes You Who You Are.* Oxford: Oxford University Press or G. Matthews, I. Deary & M. Whiteman. (2003). *Personality Traits*. Cambridge: Cambridge University Press

3 Eysenck, H. J. (1993). Creativity and personality: Suggestions for a theory. *Psychological Inquiry*, 4, 147-178 or Eysenck, H. J. (1992). The definition and measurement of psychoticism. *Personality and Individual Differences,* 13: 757-785.

ideas.[4] Rushton showed that the Big Five (and Big Three) are all co-correlated, and could all therefore be collapsed into a single personality variable, which he called the General Factor Personality (GFP).[5] GFP can be conceptualized as the single dimension of personality – from pro-social to a-social – which underlies the more specific personality traits – analogously to how general intelligence or 'g' underlies all the specific cognitive abilities, something which we explore below

So General Factor of Personality can be conceptualized as the degree to which a personality is *prosocial*– in other words, the degree to which someone has the kind of personality type and behaviours that underpin many socially desirable traits, the degree to which someone approximates to the type of person that makes for friendliness, helpfulness, being a 'good neighbour'; for peaceful, orderly, cooperative, hard-working, placid citizens.

---

[4] See, Nyborg, H. (2015). Obituary: J. Philippe Rushton: Eminent scientist, hero and friend died 2nd October 2012. In H. Nyborg (Ed). *The Life History Approach to Human Differences: A Tribute to J. Philippe Rushton.* London: Ulster Institute for Social Research.

[5] Rushton, J. P., Bons, T. A., & Hur, Y.-M. (2008). The genetics and evolution of a general factor of personality. *Journal of Research in Personality*, 42, 1173–1185 or Rushton, J. P. & Irwing, P. (2008). A General Factor of Personality from two meta-analyses of the Big Five. *Personality and Individual Differences,* 45: 679-683.

GFP describes a basic personality dimension, high levels of which (it is suggested) evolved as an adaptation in complex and stable societies so that people would 'get along together'. So a person with high GFP would be sociably extraverted, be empathic and concerned with the feelings of others, conscientious and self-disciplined in pursuit of socially-approved goals, have stable emotions, and be open to new ideas.

Marvellous as the high GFP person sounds, throughout this book we argue that a personality of almost the opposite type is necessary for the true genius (not the only thing required, but necessary) – we call this the Endogenous personality, and this new concept will soon be described in detail.

But in summary, the Endogenous personality, necessary for genius, is self-sufficient, indifferent to the opinions of others or normal social aims, being instead wrapped-up in his own personal goals, and making judgements using his own internal, subjective evaluation systems – he will work very hard and for long periods on his own projects, but will not willingly go-along with other people's plans and schemes. But more on this later...

Personality traits, depending on how they are measured, have been shown to be in the region of 50% to around 70% heritable, based mainly on twin and adoption studies.[6] (Heritability is a measure of how closely parents resemble their children in a group study – the number refers to how closely the parents' personalities predict the child's – heritability of one would mean that children's personalities were wholly a product of their parents' personalities; zero would mean the mathematical relationship between parent and offspring's personalities was random.)

Since the heritability of personality is less than one, some combination of chance and the environment does affect the kind of personality which you develop, but only within certain genetic limits. An unstable, dangerous childhood will tend to increase mental instability, and those who experience it will learn to see the world as a dangerous place – and this may have a lasting effect on their behaviour (this calibration of adult behaviour to childhood environment is the subject of Life History studies in biology – humans as well as animals).[7]

For instance, when childhood is unpredictable and dangerous, children will tend to be calibrated to

---

[6] See, Lynn, R. (2011). *Dysgenics: Genetic Deterioration in Modern Populations.* London: Ulster Institute for Social Research.

[7] Simonton, D. (2009). Varieties of (scientific) creativity: A hierarchical model of domain-specific disposition, development, and achievement. *Perspectives on Psychological Science*, 4: 441-452.

'live for the now,' so displaying lower Conscientiousness, and they may be suspicious of other people, leading to lower Agreeableness.

Another example is that girls who have grown up in sexually-unstable situations seem to adopt a short-termist sexual strategy, having children with a variety of men who are chosen for their dominance (hence probably good genes) rather than their ability to remain committed to a relationship and provide resources over the long term. In slang terms, girls from unstable homes may exhibit a preference for 'cads' rather than 'Dads'.[8]

Intelligence

So much for personality, what then is intelligence?

'Intelligence' can be seen as the ability to think abstractly and to learn quickly – this leads to an ability to solve problems quickly, but only when those problems have previously been encountered. In problem solving, intelligence provides fast processing and a larger knowledge base, but intelligence is *not* about being original or creative.

Intelligence is measured by IQ tests (meaning Intelligence Quotient; see below) and IQ test scores

---

[8] Bugental, D., Corpuz, R. & Beaulieu, D. (2014). An Evolutionary Approach to Socialization. In J. Grusec & P. Hastings (Eds). *Handbook of Socialization: Theory and Research.* Guildford Publications.

in childhood will predict many important things – higher intelligence predicts higher education level, higher socio-economic status, higher salary, better health, greater civic participation,[9] lower impulsivity, and longer lifespan[10]; lower intelligence predicts higher criminality, and (probably causally related to crime) shorter-term future-orientation.[11]

In general, therefore, high intelligence predicts desirable outcomes – however there is one important exception: high intelligence, in modern societies, predicts lower fertility – especially among women. Thus, in modern societies (with access to birth control) the most intelligent women average less than one child, because so many intelligent women have zero children, and very few have large families.[12]

Some people argue for a broader or multiple definition of intelligence, including 'emotional

---

[9] Deary, I., Batty, G. D. & Gales, C. (2008). Childhood intelligence predicts voter turnout, voter preferences and political involvement in adulthood; the 1970 cohort. *Intelligence,* 36: 548-555.

[10] For a more detailed discussion of these associations, see, Lynn R. & Vanhanen, T. (2012). *Intelligence: A Unifying Construct for the Social Sciences.* London: Ulster Institute for Social Research.

[11] Shamosh, N. A. & Gray, J. R. (2008). Delay discounting and intelligence: a meta-analysis. *Intelligence*, 36: 289-305.

[12] See Lynn, R. (2011). *Dysgenics: Genetic Deterioration in Modern Populations.* London: Ulster Institute for Social Research.

intelligence' for example. But there is, in general, no need to separate this from 'intelligence' as we define it. The ability to solve social problems has been shown to be predicted by intelligence; and all cognitive aptitudes always co-correlate in rigorous group studies, even though individuals (including geniuses) may show significantly divergent specific cognitive strengths and weaknesses.[13]

Intelligence is measured by IQ tests. These typically measure three forms of intelligence: verbal, numerical (mathematical) and spatial (geometric). Some individual people are higher in one form of intelligence than another, and rarely they may have above average measures in one measure of intelligence and below average in another – but, overall, in group studies all of the many different measures of cognitive ability (vocabulary, general knowledge, reading ability, puzzle solving, algebra, what-comes-next sequences of numbers or of symbols etc.) will always positively correlate. It is consistently found that, within-groups and between-groups, high ability in one task goes with high ability in other tasks, and *vice versa*.

This is why intelligence is called 'general', and why it can be compared with processing speed in a

[13] Kaufman, S., DeYoung, C., Reiss, D. & Gray, J. (2011). General intelligence predicts reasoning ability for evolutionarily familiar content. *Intelligence,* 39: 311-322.

computer – a 'faster' processing computer is better at doing almost every kind of task – *all* the types of software (graphics, statistics, word processing etc.) will run more efficiently. And not only does a fast computer complete tasks more quickly, but a fast computer can also do things that are – in practice – impossible for a slower computer (which will be unable to cope with the load and sequence of computations, and will 'seize-up'.).

The positive correlation between cognitive measures means that we can talk about a 'general factor' that underpins all of them. The IQ is a statistical construct which measures an inferred ability which underlies all of these cognitive abilities. This underlying ability is known as 'g' for 'general intelligence.'

Intelligence increases throughout childhood and decreases from middle age onwards (probably from early adulthood, but slowly) and, as such, IQ is usually a comparative measure – comparing the individual with a group sample of the same age. The IQ number is a way of expressing the individual's position in a rank ordering of IQ test scores for his age group; hence the term 'intelligence quotient' (IQ) (the average IQ is called 100, often calibrated against the UK population average), larger numbers are above average intelligence and lower numbers are below average (expressing this in percentage terms based on a normal distribution curve with a standard deviation of (usually) 15 IQ points – for instance an IQ above 120 is approximately in the top ten per cent of the population; and 130 in the top two per cent).

It is very important to recognise that IQ is therefore a comparative measure – and this limits its usefulness – because intelligence in a person or group is being measured only *relative* to another person or group.

The results of IQ tests strongly correlate with intuitive measures of thinking ability (such as school work) and they are not merely culturally influenced (although, naturally, culture and familiarity do have some influence). We know that IQ testing is valid and robust across cultures, because the cultures (or sub-cultures) that do badly in IQ tests do the least-badly on the most culturally-biased parts of the test, and also because the IQ test results correlate positively with something objective – that is, with differences in simple reaction times.[14]

---

[14] For a more detailed introduction to intelligence see, Dutton, E. (2014). *Religion and Intelligence: An Evolutionary Analysis.* London: Ulster Institute for Social Research, Ch. 4; Neisser, U. et al. (1996). Intelligence: knowns and unknowns. *American Psychologist*, 51: 77-101; Eysenck, H. J. (1992). *Know Your Own IQ.* London: Penguin; Jensen, A. R. (1998). *The g Factor: The Science of Mental Ability.* Westport: Praeger. For 'reaction times' and intelligence see, Jensen, A. R. (2006). *Clocking the Mind: Mental Chronometry and Individual Differences.* New York: Elsevier. For cultural bias see,

The correlation between intelligence and reaction times means that intelligence is a good indicator of how well the nervous system is running.

As already noted, intelligence is a vital predictor of life outcomes. Approximately 70% of the variance in school performance is explained by differences in intelligence, 50% of the variance among university undergraduate performance and 40% of the variance in postgraduate performance. Intelligence explains about 30% of the variance in salary and is a clear predictor of job status.[15]

It has been found that less-selective professionals, like teachers and nurses, have an IQ of about 110, while it is 120 for doctors and lawyers, and even higher for those who rise to the top of these professions.[16] Within academia, the average PhD student in education has an IQ of around 117, while the average PhD student in Physics has an IQ of 130.[17]

Jensen, A. (2015). Rushton's Contributions to the Study of Mental Ability. In H. Nyborg (Ed). *The Life History Approach to Human Differences: A Tribute to J. Philippe Rushton.* London: Ulster Institute for Social Research.

[15] Jensen, A. R. (1981). *Straight Talk About Mental Tests.* New York: Free Press.

[16] Herrnstein, R. & Murray, C. (1994). *The Bell Curve: Intelligence and Class Structure in American Life.* New York: Free Press.

[17] Harmon, L. R. 1961. "The High School Background of Science Doctorates: A Survey Reveals the Influence of Class

As with personality, intelligence is strongly heritable – indeed the heritability measures are higher for intelligence than personality, perhaps because IQ is a more precise and valid measure than are personality ratings. Around 80% of the variance in intelligence is probably genetic – overwhelmingly, therefore, intelligence is inherited from parents.[18]

Environmental factors include sufficient nutrition and a sufficiently intellectually stimulating environment when growing up. Just as important is an intellectually stimulating adult environment, which those with high intelligence will tend to create for themselves. For this reason, among others, the genetic component of IQ during childhood is relatively low, as the child's environment will reflect its parents' intelligence. Only as the child reaches adulthood will its environment reflect its own intelligence, leading to a genetic component of 80%.[19]

High intelligence is a sign of having an overall-efficient, fast-processing brain – requiring (as American psychologist Geoffrey Miller has pointed-

Size, Region of Origin, as Well as Ability, in PhD Production." *Science* 133: 679–688.

[18] Lynn, R. (2011). *Dysgenics: Genetic Deterioration in Modern Populations.* London: Ulster Institute for Social Research.

[19] Bouchard, T. J. (1998). Genetic and environmental influences on adult intelligence and special mental abilities. *Human Biology,* 70: 257-279.

out) 'good genes'; which mostly means a minimal load of deleterious mutations.[20]

Deleterious genetic mutations occur spontaneously in every generation – due to any cause of mutation (radiation, chemical, heat etc.) or from DNA copying errors – and some non-lethal but potentially-damaging mutated genes are usually inherited from parents. Nearly all chance gene mutations are harmful – and only very rarely are they 'adaptive' and improving of function (but it is these very rare beneficial mutations that are the basis of evolution by natural selection).[21]

In general, however, spontaneous mutations reduce 'fitness' (i.e. reduce reproductive potential, by damaging heritable genetic quality) and the human species has needed to prevent mutations from accumulating every generation as inherited mutations are added-to by new mutations. Somehow, these mutations need to be continually removed from the human population, or else they would overwhelm and destroy the species in a process termed Mutational Meltdown. Thus, following Miller, we would expect the more intelligent to have bodies – and especially nervous systems – that function particularly well and

---

[20] Miller, G. (2000). *The Mating Mind: How Sexual Choice Shaped the Evolution of Human Nature*. New York: Knopf.
[21] See, Hamilton, W. (1996). *The Narrow Roads of Gene Land.* Oxford: Oxford University Press.

especially in certain specific respects. For example, a high functioning nervous system has been shown to be associated with a more efficient and stronger immune response.[22]

The difference between intelligence and IQ

The difference between intelligence and IQ is that intelligence is the real, underlying psychological function, whereas IQ is a score achieved in a test – a score which is intended to compare and measure intelligence but which is an indirect, only partly-precise and only partly-valid measure of intelligence. The IQ test is clearly a sound measure of intelligence – because IQ scores correlate with other measures of cognitive problem solving ability and thus brain functioning – but it is imperfect, meaning other factors than intelligence can impact the score. In much the same way, a bathroom scales measures weight – its results correlate with other measures of weight – but some scales are better than others and no scales is perfect.

Therefore, we can think of a qualitative, subjective understanding of the phenomenon of real intelligence *as an irreducible entity* – not understood in

---

[22] Kox, M., Eijk, L, Zwaag, J. et al. (2014). Voluntary activation of the sympathetic nervous system and attenuation of the innate immune response in humans. *Proceedings of the National Academy of Sciences of the United States of America,* 20: 7379-84.

terms of other things nor only in terms of what it *does*, but in terms of itself as *a real thing* which we can detect and measure only indirectly. And we can then conceptualize IQ as the practical, simplified, publicly-shareable way of conceptualizing and investigating intelligence.

IQ can be, and usually is, researched in a 'theory-free' fashion, with operational definitions based on proxy description, measurement by comparison, and correlation – indeed intelligence is sometimes asserted to be nothing-more than a mathematical-derivation from IQ scores.

But we would emphasize that to understand intelligence requires understanding that sometimes a person *may* be of high intelligence and *not* have a similarly high IQ score (in other words, their IQ score is under-estimating their intelligence) – and that this may be the case no matter how validly, how often and how carefully the IQ is measured and calculated. And another person may have high IQ scores, measured in the best ways and by the best methods, yet *not* be of similarly high intelligence (in other words, their IQ score is *over*-estimating their intelligence).

Highly intelligent people who do *not* score as highly on IQ tests are easy to understand – because anything which reduces test performance could lead to this outcome: illness, pain, impaired consciousness and impaired concentration from sleepiness, drugs, drug-withdrawal, mental illness ... there are multiple causes, and some are chronic (long-lasting, perhaps life-long).

And people with high IQ scores who are *not* of similarly high intelligence to their scores are familiar to anyone who has attended a highly-selective college or educational programme or who are members of intellectually 'elite' professions; since they typically make-up a large proportion of participants. The 'Flynn Effect,' named after its discoverer New Zealand psychologist James Flynn, refers to the phenomenon of rising average IQ scores over the twentieth century in Western countries. The fact that this has taken place in a context of declining average real-intelligence means that the Flynn Effect can indeed be understood as evidence that IQ tests measure issues other than just intelligence, meaning they are imperfect.

(Plus, even the most reliable IQ test only has a reliability of about 0.9 when retesting the same person.)

One possible explanation for the Flynn Effect, proposed by Flynn himself, is that modern society – due to higher levels of education in the general population – makes us think in a more scientific way and this ability is partially a reflection of intelligence and partially of a separate ability that does not rely on intelligence.[23] As such, IQ tests can be used to compare intelligence within a current population but they cannot be used as easily to make comparisons over time because they are examinations and people will tend to get better at them by practicing them and thinking in the way that permits optimum performance in them as society becomes more educated. So, up to a point, IQ scores may increase over time, despite the fact that intelligence is decreasing.

After (probably) six or eight generations of rising average IQ scores and falling real-general intelligence; there has been a progressive breakdown in the strength of correlation between intelligence measured in terms of IQ scores, and intelligence understood as a real underlying, brain functional phenomenon. Indeed, it seems likely that many or most people among modern high IQ scorers do *not* have similarly high real-intelligence. This would be expected to apply especially at highly-educationally-selective institutions where Endogenous personalities are substantially selected-out by the decades-long trend for an increasingly-high minimum-threshold of conscientiousness imposed by educational qualifications.

---

[23] Flynn, J. (2012). *Are We Getting Smarter? Rising IQ in the Twenty-First Century*. Cambridge: Cambridge University Press.

The correlation between IQ score and 'g' was probably much higher in the past (a century plus ago) than it is now – meaning that the distinction between IQ score and real, underlying intelligence is more important now than it used to be.

The evolution of higher intelligence

Geoffrey Miller's emphasis on intelligence (he emphasizes particularly 'creative' intelligence) providing a 'fitness measure' which one person can evaluate in another; and his noting that relative IQ provides a quantitative correlate of deleterious mutations – is worth pausing over and amplifying.

This implies that high IQ serves as a kind-of guarantee and advertisement of 'good genes' – and this is why high intelligence is regarded as attractive, and therefore why men and women of higher intelligence tend to pair-up in marriage in much the same way that good-looking men and women tend to pair-up (this system of like pairing with like is termed 'assortative mating').

We have already noted that intelligence correlates with fast reaction times. This strongly implies that 'intelligence' is simply the function of a brain that is working well, just as strength is the function of muscle that is working well. The human body has evolved to work optimally well in a particular environment and the same is true of the human brain. Detailed historical research by British economist Gregory Clark has shown that until the Industrial Revolution a form of natural selection was operating in Western societies. Those who were not physically strong, who did not have strong immune systems, who were of low intelligence and unable to work steadily for long hours would usually either die as children or be unable to raise children of their own; and would thus be unable to pass on their deleterious genes.[24]

In other words, until about 1800 only the minority of people with (on average) the 'best genes' (i.e. the lowest mutation load) would be able to survive and reproduce; and among the great majority of the population only a very small proportion of their offspring (averaging much less than two, probably less than one, per woman) would survive to a healthy adulthood, reproduce and raise children of their own. In this context, which was for almost all of human history until about two hundred years ago; both new and inherited deleterious mutations were filtered-out, or *purged*, from the population every generation by this very harsh form of natural selection.

---

[24] Clark, G. (2007). *A Farewell to Alms: A Brief Economic History of the World.* Princeton, NJ: Princeton University Press. Clark does not explicitly mention 'intelligence' but this is precisely what is entailed by the mass of evidence he cites.

In much the same way, the number of surviving offspring was predicted by socioeconomic status – and especially by intelligence – in pre-Industrial Europe. Clark shows that in seventeenth century England, for example, the richer 50% of those who left wills had 40% higher completed fertility (children of their own, still alive when they passed away) than did the poorer 50%. In essence, the English intellectual middle classes (e.g. senior clerks, merchants, lawyers, churchmen, physicians etc.) and upper class seem to have been the most successful at reproducing for several hundred years – providing the majority of viable children with each generation so that over many generations their descendants (inheriting their ancestors' high intelligence) expanded as a proportion to become almost all of the English population.

Those with the lowest levels of deleterious mutations would, *for that reason*, have high intelligence and a high functioning immune system. As such, they would attain or maintain high socioeconomic status, and, in a context of limited medicine, their offspring would be more likely to survive. In addition, genes for intelligence would permit them to become wealthier, meaning they could better protect themselves, and their offspring, from disease, poor living conditions and accidents; and they could afford to have large numbers of children (ensuring at least some survived), without risking starvation. These two related processes would ensure that the children of the richer survived better.

The message seems to be that in pre-industrial Europe (before about 1800-1850) natural selection on humans operated mostly via mortality rates – especially child mortality rates. An average of more than half of children would die before adulthood, but this consisted of near total mortality rates among the children of the poor, and ill, and of low intelligence or 'feckless' personality; whereas among the skilled middle classes (clerks, merchants, lawyers, doctors etc.) the mortality rates were lower and fertility (number of births) was high. Therefore in each generation most of the children came from the most intelligent group in the population, and over several generations almost all the population would have been children whose ancestors were the most intelligent (also conscientious, and relatively peaceful) sector of the population.

(This is why anyone English who has ever traced their family tree will find that by the sixteenth century – when records begin – their ancestors are, at the very least, wealthy though non-aristocratic farmers ('yeomen' or richer 'husbandmen').[25] And this is why every English

---

[25] See, Dutton, E. (October 2013). So were your ancestors wealthy? *Family Tree.*

person alive is descended from King Edward III –
1312-1377).[26]

Clark argues that this harsh natural selection
resulted in an increase of average intelligence with
every generation, and ultimately culminated in the
intellectual and social breakthroughs of the
Industrial Revolution. It meant that there was a
large percentage of the society whose intelligence
was so high that the necessary breakthroughs could
be made, and that the society as a whole was
sufficiently intelligent such that it could maintain
and even develop these breakthroughs. Furthermore,
the workforce developed a personality type which
was pre-adapted (by preceding Medieval natural
selection, operating over several hundred years) to
the needs of large scale industry and complex social
organization.

The ending of selection for higher intelligence

This 'eugenic' (i.e. genetic-quality, or 'fitness'-
increasing) environment rapidly stopped in the
wake of the Industrial Revolution, and soon went
into reverse; with socioeconomic status becoming
negatively associated with fertility, especially
among women. In other words, after the Industrial

---

[26] Millard, A. (2010). Probability of descending from Edward
III.https://community.dur.ac.uk/a.r.millard/genealogy/EdwardI
IIDescent.php. Durham University.

Revolution the direction of natural selection turned upside-down, with higher social status, wealth and education leading to lower reproductive success.

This process – known as dysgenics (i.e. selection that is reducing 'fitness' – in the sense of heritable genetic quality, where deleterious mutations are taken as an index of low heritable quality hence fitness) – has been documented by British psychologist Richard Lynn. In addition, Lynn notes that the pattern of reproduction ceased to eliminate genes that would lead to a poor immune system or various physical impairments. Modern medicine means that genetically-damaged people can procreate leading to a dysgenic impact on health, more deleterious genes and thus a further negative impact on intelligence.[27]

Probably the most significant impact of the Industrial Revolution was in reducing child mortality rates from more than half to (eventually) just about one per cent. For the first time in history, almost all the population, including the poorest classes and those with the heaviest mutation loads, were leaving behind more than two surviving children. Over a few generations, the mutational load must have accumulated – fitness must have declined – and average intelligence must have

---

[27] Lynn, R. (2011). *Dysgenics: Genetic Deterioration in Modern Populations.* London: Ulster Institute for Social Research.

reduced due to the effects of deleterious mutations on brain development and functioning.

Since intelligence is correlated with genetic quality, this inferred population level mutation accumulation implies that average intelligence should have declined since the Industrial Revolution.

The inferred decline in general intelligence due to both mutation accumulation plus 'dysgenic' patterns of fertility, can be measured using simple reaction times, which correlate with 'g' – and it has been found that reaction times have slowed considerably since the late 1800s when reaction times measurements were first performed.

We will return to discuss this matter further – but so far it seems that intelligence first increased due to natural selection in the Medieval era; then has declined due to the changes in natural selection at the time of the Industrial Revolution.

So, what about personality – how was personality affected by natural selection on the European population, first in the Medieval era, then through the Industrial Revolution?

In sum, it seems that Medieval Europe was a breeding ground for high intelligence – which is one component of genius; but also a breeding ground for pro-social extraverted people of stable 'high GFP' personality type, high in conscientiousness, empathic; obedient, good at working regular hours and getting along with their neighbours.

However, although high intelligence is a component of genius, and although an average pro-social personality type is useful, and perhaps essential, for successful industrial societies; the high GFP/ pro-social personality is almost the *opposite* of that required to make a genius. And yet, late Medieval and Renaissance Europe was a veritable hotbed of genius, and it was these geniuses who enabled and triggered the Industrial Revolution.

So, how can the average population increase in pro-social personality, yet that same population generate individuals of exceptionally high intelligence who have the 'asocial' Endogenous personality type, some of whom made major breakthroughs and became recognized as geniuses?

Two ways of being highly intelligent; Good genes or the Endogenous personality

Most people would probably say that an Endogenous personality was a matter of sheer chance – that in a population characterized by high GFP, a few individuals just happened (by random variation) to have low GFP – and this low GFP/ Endogenous personality group included some individuals of very high intelligence who were the potential geniuses.

But our suggestion is different: picking-up on a suggestion from British psychologist Michael A. Woodley, we suggest that the high rate of European genius was not an accident. We will argue that the Medieval European population was under group selection as well as individual natural selection – and specifically that it was group selection which led to the evolution of geniuses.

In a nutshell, the Endogenous personality evolved in a high intelligence population to provide a significant minority of geniuses, whose function was to be specialists in creative problem solving and invention. The activities of this minority of geniuses had disproportionate impact, and were of general benefit to the survival and /or expansion of the social group among whom the geniuses lived and worked.

Indeed, we would argue that there are two ways of being exceptionally intelligent. The usual way is that someone in a population is exceptionally intelligent is by what is termed Good Genes: that is, having few genetic faults or errors – the person has a structurally normal brain, but with nothing (or nothing much) wrong with it. In other words he has a low load of deleterious mutations (or, conversely, he is *not* suffering from mutation accumulation).

But there is another way – which is by having an Endogenous personality – which means that his brain is purposely *designed* (by group selection –

the mechanisms of which are currently poorly understood) to be creative, to make breakthroughs. Such a person is, in sum, a genius (albeit very probably *not* a world historical genius; but a tribal or local genius).

Our assumption is that in the potential genius – and if we could measure it, which is not possible at present – we would see a brain *wired-up to be intelligent* and not merely intelligent, but also wired-up to be more orientated towards internal processing – more intuitively creative, more internally-motivated.

Therefore the brain of an Endogenous personality is an *evolutionarily specialized brain*; which has high intelligence not so much negatively from lack of mutations; as positively – because it is a brain 'designed' (by natural selection) to be highly efficient for the purpose of creative discovery.

And this is why the genius has a special (Endogenous) personality. Usually personality and intelligence are almost distinct and little-correlated; but the brain of a genius is differently wired from a normal brain: it is a specialized and purposive brain, a lop-sided brain, a brain in which some circuits usually used for social intelligence and reproductive success are co-opted to serving a creative purpose.

In sum, *the brain of a genius is one that is specialized for creative discovery* and both high intelligence and an 'inner-oriented' personality are features of this specialization. This is why personality and intelligence go together in the genius, whereas in 'normal people' personality and genius can vary almost independently and there is little correlation between the two.

We have discussed, then, the concepts of personality and intelligence and the factors that lead to differences in them. We will now attempt to understand how these relate to genius.

Chapter Three

Different understandings of Genius

What is the nature of 'genius'? There are many layers to genius – although typically only those nearest the surface are considered. Some of the main layers are:

1. Sociological: Impact on history
2. Biological–differential: Reproductive Success
3. Biological–ideal: Fitness
4. Philosophical–Theological: Fitness for what? Ultimate Purpose?

Let us consider each in turn.

1. Sociological – this is the usual level of analysis, the usual definition of a genius. A genius is seen as a person who has made a disproportionately large impact on human history. This can be measured more-or-less objectively by evaluating the consensus of expert historians of science, technology, arts, literature etc. – since these experts exhibit a high level of agreement concerning what is most important.

While this is, broadly, the interpretation we use in this book with which to frame genius – the sociological category is over inclusive, since individuals may have a large impact on human history despite a non-exceptional, non-genius personality or mediocre ability; as examples due to accident of birth (e.g. some monarchs), accidents of public response (the 'famous for being famous' phenomenon), being married to a major figure and thereby having power and influence bestowed for that reason; or simply from the luck, or misfortune, of being in the right place at the right time.

2. Biological – Differential. A genius is seen in biological terms as one who makes a disproportionately large impact on human reproduction. This is measured in terms of reproductive success, which is measured in terms of the number of descendants of a genius and/or the group to which he belongs to – or, in the relevant case of group selection, biological success is measured in terms of the survival and expansion of the social group to which the genius belongs.

By this measure, a genius is one who causes a measurable increase in the numbers or proportion of his society (by some measure) – examples of such geniuses would be those who created the technical breakthroughs leading to the Agrarian and Industrial Revolutions – for example Robert Bakewell (1725-95) the animal breeder, Coke of Norfolk (Thomas Coke, Earl of Leicester, 1754-1842) the deviser of more efficient farming methods; or Richard Trevithick (1771-1833) the inventor of the high pressure steam engine.

And an 'anti-genius' would be one who did the opposite: caused a decline in the number or proportion of descendants or group members. Candidates would include Napoleon, whose policies and wars seem to have caused a collapse in the French population relative to the British one.[28]

3. Biological – Ideal. This takes account of the objective, not differential, effect of 'fitness' (here defined in terms of heritable genetic quality) by estimating organismal functionality – the reproductive potential of an average organism is a given environment.

For example, a lineage may increase in its numbers or proportion of the population; even though there is an accumulation of deleterious mutations which damage basic functionality. We would argue that this was happening in Europe among the lower classes during the 19th century. One effect of the Industrial Revolution, in Gregory Clark's work, was that the lower classes increased both numerically and as a proportion of the European population (due to maintaining high fertility as child mortality rates declined) – however,

---

[28] Mosk, C. (2013). *Nationalism and Economic Development in Modern Eurasia.* London: Routledge, p.134.

we argue that despite this 'success' the underlying fitness/genetic quality of the lower classes was actually declining, due to mutation accumulation.

So reproductive success (absolute or relative) can increase even as the underlying functionality or fitness declines. This can happen when the environment is less harsh, inflicts a lower mortality rate – as with animals in a zoo, or humans in modern society. This would be seen if the experiment was done of returning an animal, or human, to its 'wild' or original environment – when the capacity of the organism (or species) to survive and reproduce will be seen to have declined.

We assume that this has happened to modern Man in general and everywhere since the Industrial Revolution: i.e. his 'ideal' fitness has declined; and this would be seen if or when modern Man had to return to pre-1800 conditions, for example if the Industrial Revolution unravelled and the world returned to a Medieval type agrarian society.

If or when this happens, we would predict that the human population would collapse to numbers significantly *below* 1800 levels, and would stay low for several or many generations – simply because Men would be less fit, less well adapted (their adaptations having been destroyed by mutation accumulation). But this fitness decline is presently obscured by the 'softness' and abundance of modern life, which is itself a product of breakthroughs by geniuses of the past.

Thus there is a lag between the onset of mutation accumulation and the effects working their way through the population. And the inertial benefit of past geniuses continues to produce a comfortable and low-mortality environment Man for some generations after genius has itself dwindled.

4. Philosophical – Theological – Fitness for what?

If an ideal, not actual, concept of fitness is to be used, then it is not clear what the environment against which fitness or functionality should be measured is. This creates a need for, opens space for, a philosophical discourse about what Man's fitness *ought* to be.

By this account, a genius is one who enhances his group's fitness for (or functionality-in) the kind of environment which Man is *aiming-for*, or wants to have. One version of this would be a genius tending to create Men fitted for utopia. Such a definition would include philosophers in the broad sense of the word; artists, painters, poets, literary authors etc. – from Plato to Hegel and beyond.

In ultimate terms, the deepest understanding of genius is perhaps one who promotes the ultimate purpose of Life-itself, in terms of the divine plan or ultimate purpose of life. This definition would include religious founders, prophets, saints, holy men and women; and also some artists, poets, and thinkers.

Overall, it can be seen that these four definitions of genius dissociate. For example, a genius who promotes theological ultimate purpose may damage reproductive success (if a good new religious group is exterminated). A genius who promotes reproductive success may damage ideal fitness (i.e. the population increases but so does the deleterious mutation load).

In this book, we will understand 'genius' primarily in the sociological sense: that is, a world-historical genius is seen as a person who has made a disproportionately large impact on human history – but we will restrict the definition of genius to a specific psychological group within this category: thus, our concept of a genius is one who has the Endogenous personality and who, *because of this*, has made a disproportionate impact on human society and history.

Furthermore, we consider the *potential* genius to be someone who has the Endogenous personality but has not, or not yet, made a large impact; and geniuses may also be classified by the scale and depth of their impact – some with an impact that is international and permanent, some with a local and more temporary impact.

And, of course, the personal identity of a genius may or may not be known; or may be lost to history

– so we know the identity of Shakespeare who wrote the Sonnets; but the names of those geniuses who wrote the Border Ballads (coming from the Border of England and Scotland in the late Medieval era, and later recorded from oral tradition by the likes of the great novelist and poet Sir Walter Scott – 1771-1832) are all lost, and perhaps never were known.[29]

This, of course, means that, from a particular vantage point, it is possible to distinguish between the impact of a 'good' genius and an 'evil' genius' according to the nature of the socio-historical impact; and we will also consider the semi-genius or borderline genius – someone who has made a significant impact short of crossing the threshold into world historical importance.

---

[29] See Lloyd, A. (2008). *Folk Song in England.* London: Faber & Faber.

Chapter Four

The Creative Triad

The Endogenous personality, as we have discussed, refers to someone who is inner-orientated. Our suggestion is that this personality complex is associated with genuine creativity and – in rare instances, with creative genius. This raises an important question immediately. What does it mean to be creative? What is the nature of creativity?

We can conceive of a Creative Triad. It is composed of (1) Innate ability (2) Inner-motivation, and (3) Intuitive thinking. This triad is the essence of how we use the word 'creative' in everyday life. The 'creative' type is the 'arty' type: the novelist, the poet, and especially the artist; and by extension, also the truly original scientist and technological innovator.

Genius is made possible when all parts of this Triad flow together in a particular way: a person is internally-motivated to pursue that for which he has a natural ability; and does so in an "intuitive" way that mobilizes his deepest self, all his mental powers. Major genius occurs when the 'natural ability' dimension is also extremely high.

But people can still be 'creative' yet not reach the level of genius, they may be considered as semi- or borderline-genius when their historic impact on a society is real but modest. For example, there are numerous 'local geniuses' who are relative geniuses compared to those around them, and make genius type social contributions – but their impact is geographically or temporally restricted. Most geniuses are, in fact, of this type.

And, of course, a potential genius may (for reasons we will discuss later) fail to make an influential break-through or may make a breakthrough that fails to be recognized and acted-upon.

Before turning, then, to the nature of 'the creative' we need to be clear on the nature of each of its component parts and how they contribute to creativity and genius. It is clear how 'innate ability' does, but what about intuition? What is intuition?

We could approach intuition by stating that intuition is the mode of thought of the private soul/ the real self/ inner consciousness – that is to say the most profound, the most secret, fundamental mode of thought. Intuition can be contrasted with two (lower, subordinated) modes of thinking: passions versus reason; the body v the brain; gut-feelings v head-knowledge; instinct v logic. These two modes are not absolutely distinct, but we think they can usefully be distinguished.

So, what is the thought mode of intuition? It is not by instinct nor by logic – but by something of both, and more. Therefore, intuition is a mode of thinking which simultaneously uses emotion and logic but operating in a context of (for example) motivation, purpose, meaning and relationships. In a nutshell, *intuition uses all possible modes of thinking*; and this is why intuition leads to a greater feeling of sureness, of certainty, than do other, more partial forms of thought.

The result of intuition is therefore an evaluation which is uniquely convincing because it is validated by the full range of positive responses. It is an insight that satisfies both logic and reason, and also 'feels' right. By contrast, if we use only (for example) logic, or only emotions, to evaluate something; then the evaluation will be incomplete, and evaluation in one sub-mode may be contradicted by evaluation in another sub-mode – as when logic and emotions reach different conclusions, point in different directions, contradict one-another – and we feel confused or torn because our head and our heart are in conflict.

Only the evaluations of intuition are fully satisfying, fully convincing, and harmonious. Only the evaluations of intuition mobilize the whole range of thought modes. Thus *intuition is the most powerful mode of thought*, and the only mode of thought capable of mobilizing the fullest degree of motivation. Intuition is what makes us care most about ideas: it is what *engages* us with creativity. This is why intuition is necessary to the highest levels of creativity, to the greatest attainments of genius.

Our second question is: what is inner motivation and why is it necessary for creativity and genius?

The genius must combine the inner orientation of the contemplative – in order to find his own problem, the problem he is destined to work on; with an inner motivation towards action directed to solving this problem. He must desire to translate understanding into engagement; not just to contemplate reality, but to 'solve' reality.

So, something deep within the genius – and not the promise of an external reward – makes him want to fully comprehend or improve or express the nature of reality. Because his motivation comes from within, and he is focused upon a problem which also comes from within, the genius is not easily discouraged; his drive will enable him – will indeed compel him – to keep pushing and pushing, even when support is withdrawn or he is met by discouragement and failure.

Therefore – when it comes to his own problem – the genius is autonomous, self-motivating, tenacious and stubborn in pursuit of his Destiny. He will see the Genius Quest, as we might term it, through to its conclusion in Illumination or 'die in the attempt' – unless he is actively prevented from doing so.

In summary, the creative personality of a genius involves an Inner orientation which includes a basis in intuitive modes of thinking and an inner source of motivation – we will now further explore the nature of this motivation.

Chapter Five

What Motivates the Genius Quest?

The genius –has a 'journey' to make, a 'path' to take – a 'way' to live: a Quest.

Pursuing this Quest is the Destiny of the genius – it is what he is 'meant to do'.

After this, various things may happen. The Quest may be discovered and embarked upon, but there is no guarantee it will be completed. It may be tried but may fail. The genius may die, or get sick before it is finished – or in some way be thwarted or defeated. The Destiny may be accepted, but may later be abandoned; because the commitment must be renewed many times. Illumination may actually be achieved but rejected by society – the genius unrecognised. Or, Illumination may be achieved but stolen and no credit given. Or the Quest may be achieved, and the Illumination socially-accepted, and acknowledgement may even be given... but then the genius becomes corrupted into careerism, status seeking, pleasure seeking, or whatever takes him away from his Destiny.

As an example of an abandoned Quest, the mathematician and historian of science Jacob Bronowski (1908-1974) claimed, in in his 1972 TV series *The Ascent of Man*, that this was the fate of the mathematical and computing genius – and friend of Bronowski's – John von Neumann (1903-1957). Von Neumann was, late in life, lured away from focusing on his intellectual pursuits by love of power, status and prestige – leaving his work incomplete. And such was the greatness of von Neumann, that it proved difficult, indeed impossible, for anyone else to complete it. So, here was a real genius who accepted and partially-completed his unique Quest – yet without quite finishing what he began.

Psychoticism versus Openness

This emphasis on Destiny stresses that the genius has an unusual life, compared with normal people. But what does the genius get out of his unusual life?

Usually, he will simply enjoy being creative; and, indeed, being-creative will be a significant part of his sense of self, consequently he will be a noticeably different kind of person from the one whom we would see as 'conventional.'

Hans Eysenck regarded creativity as an aspect of the Psychoticism trait – indicating a particular way of thinking and relating to the world which incorporated creativity as positive, and psychotic and psychopathic traits as negative, aspects of this trait.

Working more recently, British psychologist Daniel Nettle's review of the psychological literature has shown that certain personality traits – in particular Openness-Intellect and Neuroticism – are associated with being creative, quite independent of being a highly successful creative – and indeed most personality psychologists nowadays regard Openness as the characteristic trait of a creative person.[30]

So which is the best way of conceptualizing the personality of a creative person? Is it the eccentricity and originality and semi-craziness of Psychoticism, or the novelty-generation; and clever, fashionable fertility of Openness?

This is a topic to which we will return, but in brief we favour the older concept of Psychoticism as a better description of creativity – and we have derived the Endogenous personality from Eysenck's analysis of the genius. However, we have departed from Eysenck by emphasizing that the high Endogenicity variable is rooted in group adaptiveness, and not in individual pathology. Also, we focus on a brain specialized by an innate *innerness of orientation* as the basis of the personality trait cluster; whereas Eysenck explained higher Psychoticism in terms of a broader field of associations.

Our reason for our preference and emphasis for rejecting the currently dominant explanation of

---

[30] Nettle, D. (2007). *Personality: What Makes You Who You Are.* Oxford: Oxford University Press.

creativity by Openness and our advocacy of a development of the older idea of Psychoticism; is that Openness and Psychoticism (Endogenous personality) are at opposite ends of the General Factor Personality dimension: Openness is pro-social and Psychoticism/ Endogenous is a-social.

In other words, Openness type creativity is a response from a conscientious and empathic person to social demands or needs; while Psychoticism/ Endogenous creativity comes from the inner and innate drive of someone substantially indifferent to current societal self-awareness, knowledge and roles.

As such, we would suggest that 'creative' is not what you 'do' but what you 'are.'

The satisfactions of creativity

Creative people thus reflect a certain kind of personality, leading to characteristic behaviours. But why do creative people behave creatively? What exactly do 'creatives' get out of being creative? What, in other words, is the *phenomenology* of creativity? (Note: Phenomenology refers to first-person, inner, subjective experience – how things look 'from the inside').

People could only be creative by disposition if creativity were supported with positive and rewarding emotions and/or provided relief from negative or aversive emotions. This would seem to work in three stages:

Discontent – Delight – Satisfaction

Corresponding to:

Perceiving a Problem – Having an Insight – Generating a Solution

Therefore, creativity is driven by a negative or 'Dysphoric' feeling – that some state of affairs produces an emotion of dissatisfaction. 'The creative' (as we shall term him) then turns his attention to this "problem" – and he enjoys working on the problem (that is, he enjoys '*being* creative'); and finally he may come up with an insight which leads to a euphoric feeling of delight.

So, the creative is rewarded up-front for generating insights – by working on a problem he both gets relief from a negative state of inner dissatisfaction and is also positively rewarded by an inner fulfilment by the work – and this happens whether or not his insights eventually turn-out to be answers. As such, the creative will tend to generate insights *for the sheer fun of it!* – and even if the insights turn-out to be trivial, erroneous, useless, or harmful.

But, finally, with persistence and luck on his side; let us say that the creative comes up with a solution to the problem: a solution which, for a shortish period (minutes or hours, perhaps), makes him feel joyously happy or 'Euphoric'!

Thus a Dysphoric state of Discontent has then been replaced by a Euphoric state; and when Euphoria subsides the successful creative will move onto a longer-term and sustained state of satisfaction or gratification – and this can be termed 'Euthymic', meaning a state of 'normal' good mood. Therefore, first Euphoria, then Euthymia are the emotional rewards for creativity.

So, in terms of phenomenology, it goes:

Dysphoria – Euphoria – Euthymia

Or, in English: Discontent, Bliss, Satisfaction

In terms of the larger picture of Life, this is the discontented state of seeking Destiny and the gratification of discovering it; embarking on a Quest – which is itself a satisfying albeit frustrating activity; and finally achieving Illumination – which leads to an acute state of bliss then a chronic state of satisfaction (and quite likely a new search for another Destiny).

Therefore, for the creative person, a normal life in conformity with social expectations is unsatisfying; but being creative is rewarding. Such a person will be *spontaneously* creative, as a consequence of their inner drives and personal satisfactions; and creative whether asked to be creative or not, whether it is useful or not, and whether he is sufficiently knowledgeable and competent for the task or not.

Accordingly, if real creativity is wanted or needed, then the job absolutely requires a creative person. And if you have a creative person in place, and he is sufficiently interested in what you want him to do, then he *will be* creative.

However, since creativity is inwardly generated by innate mechanisms, such creativity is not externally controllable and directable by normal social pressures, rewards, priorities. Both to get the best from a creative, and also to have that best be directed where desired, requires that the creative be animated, inspirited and energized by the task; and allowed to work in his own way.

Therefore a genius can neither be 'managed' nor 'regulated' – although he may to some extent be 'led' by a sufficiently inspiring and insightful individual

Chapter Six

Successful Creativity

Now that we have an understanding of the creative person, his personality, and what motivates him, we must tease out the difference between the 'creative' and the genius. In essence, we argue that the creative genius is *a sub-species* of the creative type, and the genuinely creative is characterized by the Endogenous personality type. So, the genius is the most successful and able and obvious type of 'creative' – and genius is an extreme form of creativity combined with other attributes (mainly exceptional ability, and especially with exceptional intelligence).

We have already proposed a correspondence between genius – understood as having an enormous impact in some field through highly original activity – and creativity. We would expect the genius to be 'creative' but there is a difference between being 'creative' (as it is commonly defined) and actually being original and insightful.

For example, people tend to think that poetry is intrinsically a creative activity – but we would emphasize that most self-styled or professionally-recognized poets are not especially creative, and that much greater creativity may be found among some people who are doing (for example) practical work, or caring for children than among the typical writer and publisher of poems.

In other words, properly understood, 'poetry' is a social function (a job, a hobby, an educational or academic task) which may be done more, or less, creatively – and this is probably the usual situation for most social roles. However, at the very highest level – a level that is at best rare and sometimes absent from society – poetry is indeed (of course!) a paradigm of creativity, and The Poet the epitome of genius.

What of originality? The originality of a creative person is likely to be achieved without being aimed at, through combining creativity with innate ability (in particular, intelligence) and a lack of concern about the reaction to one's originality. Sometimes, in honest and creative pursuit of some goal (on a Quest), you need to break conventions and rules. The reaction to that which challenges the vested interests of the *status quo* is generally negative – so creativity risks alienating powerful people and causing irritation or even hostility.

Therefore there is an *association* between creativity and originality, and between originality and offensiveness. But, on the other hand, the opposite is untrue; so, it is *not* true to say that that which causes irritation, offence and hostility is *therefore* original; nor to say that what is original is *therefore* creative.

Nonetheless, this falsely reversed causality has been the prevalent way in which creativity and originality have been identified in the modern era; for instance in the visual arts since the era of Dadaism about a century ago.[31] In *avant garde* circles, successfully provoking outrage (especially among 'respectable' people and the religious) has usually been regarded as sufficient evidence of originality, hence genius – leading to the ludicrous situation in which artistically-talentless confidence tricksters and public relations manipulators have successfully passed themselves off as artistic geniuses, and for three or four generations have dominated the professional world of Art.

Furthermore, in discussing creativity, a decision must be made as to whether we are going to give primacy to creative process or creative outcome. Not neglecting the other of the pair: but one of the two must come first.

We put process first – and therefore we discuss creativity as a disposition and process, and how these lead to what are generally regarded as creative outcomes. This opens a potential gap between creative activity and creative outcomes. So if a science Nobel Prize is regarded as a creative outcome, then we would say that some science

---

[31] For a discussion of Dada see, Richter, H. (1965). *Dada: Art and Anti-art*. Oxford: Oxford University Press

Nobel Prize winners were highly creative persons – although some were not.

Some Nobelists seemingly got the prize in other ways: for instance by stealing or otherwise getting credit for the ideas or work of other people, or by careful and conscientious work extending the creative breakthroughs of others, or by self-promotion, or from lack of any really deserving prize-winners (this, especially, in recent years – when the supply of geniuses has all-but dried-up, and science has become more bureaucratic and less creative); or simply by errors or corruption or committee-think on the part of the Nobel prize committee.

And much the same would apply to great composers, great writers, great visual artists etc.

But if, instead, creativity is defined in terms of *process*, as a mode of thinking; then this means that many or most of the people who produce work (or outcomes) that are generally regarded as extremely useful, beautiful or true – are *not* creative people.

For example, the work of British Nobelist Dorothy Hodgkin (1910-1994) was mostly a careful extension of the primary work of Desmond Bernal (1901-1971; her mentor and lover) – who was the real genius behind X-Ray Crystallography – but it was Hodgkin who did the work that got the prize. Significantly, Bernal had the classical genius temperament[32] while Hodgkin – although extremely clever and skilful – showed hardly a spark of real 'Endogenous' creativity.[33]

Furthermore, many or most creative people ('creatives') nowadays do not achieve anything that is generally regarded as useful, beautiful or true. We know of relatively unknown and unacknowledged 'creatives' who also have truly great abilities and are probably potential geniuses, but lack either the application or the luck to have made an influential breakthrough; or else their breakthroughs were not acknowledged as such. Indeed, some have suffered aggressive and harmful persecutions, such as professional harassment and mass media mobbing, for their honesty. For example, an insightful and original scientist working in an obscure branch of medicine, a major theoretician working in a field where only empirical and large scale research is valued...

Sometimes, the achievement of a genius seems to have hung by a thread; if British Nobellist and DNA-discoverer Francis Crick (1916-2004) had died at age 35, or had lived a generation later, he would have been regarded as one of these – merely a brilliant, restless, unfulfilled *dilettante*.

---

[32] Goldsmith, M. (1980). *Sage: A Life of J. D. Bernal*. London: Hutchinson.
[33] Ferry, G. (1998). *Dorothy Hodgkin A Life*. London: Granta Books.

The 'evil genius' phenomenon

It may happen that a highly creative person, by chance or design, deploys their creativity in such a way that it destroys their own field: a Picasso, a James Joyce, a Schoenberg... men of genius whose work was highly influential and brilliant, but who left their subjects and the world a worse place than they found it: they were each, artistically, a dead-end. These are versions of the 'evil genius' – so named because of their effects, rather than necessarily their motivations.

From the vantage point of creating something useful (to maintaining and developing civilization), beautiful or true, Pablo Picasso's (1881-1973) artistic philosophy involved rejecting the idea that art should create beauty and a road to transcendence. His purpose was to challenge the accepted way of doing art and so challenge all that was established, including that which is useful. In so-doing, his art created a sense of shock, confusion, and meaninglessness and contributed to anarchy.[34] The novels and stories of James Joyce (1882-1941) share much of this philosophy. *The Dubliners*, for example, horrified audiences with its detailed depictions of depraved behaviour and these

---

[34] See, Leighton, P. (2013). *The Liberation of Painting: Modernism and Anarchism in Avant Guerre Paris.* University of California Press.

actually occurring in real (named) streets and pubs. The stories take the reader into a world of nihilism and *Finnegan's Wake* simply creates a sense of 'profound' confusion.[35] As for Arnold Schoenberg (1874-1951), he shunned musical harmony and tradition in favour of a highly-structured but incomprehensible kind of music which most people find it actively-unpleasant to listen to . . . a world in which nothing makes sense, there is no meaning, there is negativity, there is the Void.[36]

So, these evil geniuses may or may not have had exceptionally wicked personalities, although all were somewhat unpleasant characters[37] – but they did have a net-destructive effect on society. This effect was net-destructive because they advanced a compelling but destructive worldview; one which led to the suppression of, for example, the ability of people to perceive meaning and purpose in life, or active-encouragement of selfish, parasitic, or cruel behaviour.

Other examples might be philosophers such as Rousseau, Marx or Nietzsche.[38] From the vantage

---

[35] See: Cotton, D. (2003). *James Joyce and the Perverse Ideal.* London: Psychology Press.

[36] See: MacDonald, M. (2008). *Schoenburg.* Oxford: Oxford University Press.

[37] Picasso possessed almost every symptom of psychopathic personality, for example.

[38] See, Dutton, E. & van der Linden, D. (2015). Who are the 'Clever Sillies'? The intelligence, personality, and motives of

point already outlined, the philosophy of Jean-Jacques Rousseau (1712-1778) rejected civilization in favour of a more 'natural' life modelled on a romantic-ideal of the tribe in which all were supposedly equal and free. This would be a dictatorship of 'the people' in which dissent, however, could not be tolerated; with dissenters labelled (in the Rousseau-influenced French Revolution) as 'enemies of the people.'

Karl Marx's (1818-1883) philosophy – heavily influenced by Rousseau – altered the idealized group from the 'tribe' to the 'worker' and argued that a worker's dictatorship must inevitably develop to ensure equality based on Marx's fate-based understanding of History. Again, dissent was not to be permitted and dissenters were 'enemies,' 'imperialists' and so on. Its culmination was the world-historical horror of twentieth century Communism, and its descendant Political Correctness, in which 'the worker' is replaced by supposedly oppressed or more natural 'cultural' groups. Dissenters are 'racist' and other catch-all, highly emotive terms (such as 'hater' or 'denialist')

---

clever silly originators and those who follow them. *Intelligence*, 49: 57-65. On Nietzsche, see, Kaufmann, W. (1974). *Nietzsche: Philosopher, Psychologist, Antichrist*. Princeton: Princeton University Press. On Marx see, Sowell, T. (1986). *Marxism*. New York: HarperCollins. On Rousseau, see, Damrosch, L. (2007). *Jean-Jacques Rousseau: Restless Genius*. London: Houghton, Mifflin, Harcourt.

employed to discourage dissent, such that even the slightest deviance from orthodoxy is termed 'racist' in order to reprove it and intimidate the deviant into silence.[39] These ideologies can distilled down to three essential dogmas: (1) Those who have power – whether financial or cultural and whether deserved or not – are bad and should repent by giving it to those who lack power and creating 'equality' (2) Those who lack power – on whatever measure is seen as important – are superior to those who have it because they are somehow more genuine and (3) Those who dissent from this view are wicked. As such, the dogma of 'equality' serves to create a 'thought prison' which would be antithetical to genius and, in both cases, the desires of a 'natural group' must be put before all else, including making the decisions required to maintain civilization.

Multiculturalism is related to Political Correctness, arguing that Western countries benefit from disempowering their cultural majority in favour of a cultural melting pot, and systematically

---

[39] See: For examinations of Political Correctness see: Ellis, F. (2004). *Political Correctness and the Theoretical Struggle: From Lenin and Mao to Marcuse and Foucault.* Auckland: Maxim Institute; Dutton, E. (2012). *Culture Shock and Multiculturalism.* Newcastle: Cambridge Scholars Publishing; or Charlton, B. G. (2011). *Thought Prison: The Fundamental Nature of Political Correctness.* Buckingham: Buckingham University Press.

privileging non-native ethnic groups. This is underpinned by cultural and moral relativism; and this brings us to the genius of F. W. Nietzsche (1844-1900).

Nietzsche's work is complex, self-contradictory, evolving; esoteric and brilliant in style, of superb literary quality and shot-through with memorable, incisive insights. Nonetheless the *net* effect of Nietzsche has been bad. He argued for a kind of moral and cultural relativism, or even a moral inversion by which traditional human values are reversed: what was evil becomes good and *vice versa*. The basic idea was that people in general, and the natural leaders of 'Supermen' in particular, should pursue their wild, instinctive, amoral dominant desires, helping them to be creative, life-affirming and to experience the heights of ecstasy. In *Beyond Good and Evil,* he clearly advocates moral relativism, arguing that what is 'moral' depends on whether you are a 'master' or a 'servant.' In *The Anti-Christ,* it is argued that the only 'good' is the gaining of power. So, in essence, Nietzsche advocates living an utterly selfish life in pursuit of one's own power. Clearly, if everyone lived in such a way civilization would collapse and there would be no room to philosophize at all.[40]

---

[40] For a more detailed summary of Nietzsche's philosophy see: Leiter, B. (2015). Nietzsche's Moral and Political Philosophy. In *Stanford Encyclopedia of Philosophy,*

On top of this; Nietzsche's sister edited, emphasized and altered his works to make them even more appealing to the embryonic National Socialists – eventually the Nazis came to regard his *Thus Spake Zarathustra* as an equivalent of the Bible, and issued tens of thousands of copies to soldiers for their spiritual guidance… On the one hand, there is no doubt that Nietzsche himself would strongly have disapproved of this; on the other hand, it does not require much in the way of selection and distortion to extract Nazism from Nietzsche.

So it is not necessarily a compliment to call somebody creative or 'a creative' – really, it is simply a *description* of a personality type.

Once we understand genius or high impact originality in terms of achievement, then there is a clear quantitative basis for asserting that a relationship exists between this and being disagreeable; and it is this combination of creativity, ability and being disagreeable which can lead to genius. American psychologist Dean Simonton has conducted a great deal of research on this subject and has found that academics who are considered

---

http://plato.stanford.edu/contents.html#n *'Moral and Political Philosophy'* (Accessed 15 August 2015).

highly original – and, indeed, recognized geniuses – tend to have distinctive personality features.[41]

According to Simonton, geniuses usually have a personality type characterized by moderately high Psychoticism; that is: a psychosis-/ dream-like mode of thinking; indifference to public opinion; moderately low Agreeableness/ Empathizing and moderately low Conscientiousness. This, according to Simonton, is usually combined with high Openness-Intellect (strongly associated with creativity), and high Neuroticism (in the case of artistic geniuses) and high Extraversion (in the case of scientific geniuses).

As a reminder, we argue that this rather vague and complex constellation of statistical associations between traits can more parsimoniously, and validly, be conceptualized as the Endogenous personality. Furthermore, we will look below at how high levels of Neuroticism and Extraversion may actually be an artefact, due to the only-approximate validity of measuring what are inferred to be dispositional traits in terms of overt behaviour.

Both genius artists and scientists in turn combine this kind of personality with extremely

---

[41] Simonton, D. (2009). Varieties of (scientific) creativity: A hierarchical model of domain-specific disposition, development, and achievement. *Perspectives on Psychological Science*, 4, 441-452; Simonton, D. (1988). *Genius, creativity and leadership.* Cambridge, MA: Harvard University Press.

high – outlier levels of – intelligence. Outlier intelligence occurs when chance combinations of genes in relatively intelligent parents lead to extreme intelligence in one of the offspring. Most children have intelligence at a similar level to the average of their parents; but it is quite possible for children to be far more – or less – intelligent than their parents, though this is rare. It is even rarer, though still possible, that average or even below average parents could produce a highly intelligent child.

Therefore genius is most frequently found among offspring of the most intelligent people, but can be found almost anywhere, albeit at lower frequencies.

This seems difficult to explain in the way that intelligence is normally considered – in terms of intelligence being a consequence of very large numbers (thousands?) of genes-for-intelligence. With intelligence genes conceptualized as additive in effect, and in such large numbers, it is hard to understand how a very highly intelligent child could emerge by chance from low-intelligence parents. But if a person's level of intelligence is also determined by the number of deleterious mutations they inherit from their parents, and these mutations are numbered in tens – then it is imaginable that, by chance, a child may be born with very few deleterious mutations, despite his parents having a relatively heavy mutation load.

This notion is perhaps testable, on the basis that a low mutation load should be associated with generally higher fitness, and therefore with traits associated with high fitness – so the high intelligence child of low intelligence parents would be expected to be (on average) taller, healthier, more symmetrical, and more long-lived than his low intelligence parents.

The face and body have evolved to be symmetrical. Thus, facial symmetry shows that relatively few genetic mutations, which are almost always negative, have been inherited. It also shows that a symmetrical phenotype has been maintained in the face of disease, implying a genetically good immune system. Symmetrical people are, therefore, regarded as attractive because their appearance advertises their genetic good health.[42] Studies have actually shown a weak positive correlation between intelligence and facial symmetry.[43]

But, although highly intelligent children of less-intelligent parents have been, by chance, spared from the effects of deleterious mutations *on the*

---

[42] Scheib, J., Gangestad, S. & Thornhill, R. (1999). Facial attractiveness, symmetry and cues to good genes. *Proceedings of the Royal Society of London,* B 266: 1913-1917.

[43] E.g. Kanazawa, S. (2011). Intelligence and physical attractiveness. *Intelligence,* 39: 7-14.

brain; nonetheless they would be likely to be carrying more deleterious mutations than the highly intelligent children of highly intelligent parents (because not all mutations affect the brain). So among the highly intelligent children of less intelligent parents, there might be evidence of relatively higher levels of other mutation-related dysfunctions – e.g. social maladaptiveness, psychosexual dysfunctions, psychiatric problems, fluctuating asymmetry or physical illnesses with a genetic basis.

It should also be noted that intelligence affects behaviour. High intelligence may act as a counterbalance to a personality type that would otherwise be associated with asocial behaviours characteristic of low General Factor of Personality (GFP). High IQ in a low GFP person provides a strong future orientation and self-control – due to a heightened ability to predict the consequences of their actions and a greater concern with the long-term[44] – that such individuals would otherwise lack from their inherited personality traits.

Whereas with high intelligence a low GFP person may be merely a-social –uninterested by society; low GFP person and low intelligence might

---

[44] The association between intelligence and time preference has been shown in, Shamosh, N. A. & Gray, J. R. (2008). Delay discounting and intelligence: a meta-analysis. *Intelligence*, 36: 289-305.

well be *anti*-social – that is, significantly hostile, or actively socially destructive in their behaviour.

Chapter Seven

Identifying the Genius

When genius is defined as a type of person who evolved to benefit the group (by innovatively being able to solve novel problems and enhance social cohesion, survival and population growth), it can be understood that it is beneficial for societies to be able to *recognize and identify* potential geniuses; so that they may be helped, tolerated; or at the least not actively attacked and suppressed.

But there has long been a confusion or blurring of the genius personality type with psychosis – with insanity: as in the phrase of English poet John Dryden (1631-1700): "Great wits to madness sure are near allied, and thin partitions do their bounds divide". Furthermore, there is a relatively higher incidence of some forms of madness (especially melancholia and mania) and also alcoholism and drug abuse among geniuses and other creative people than among comparable control subjects.[45]

Yet we argue that creativity is not caused by madness, not even by partial degrees of psychosis – rather we argue that most madness is utterly uncreative, being maladaptive and caused by

---

[45] Storr, A. (1972). *The Dynamics of Creation*. London: Penguin.

accidental pathology; while the root of creativity is to be found in the Endogenous personality, which is an adaptation that evolved to perform a valuable social function.

However, and this is a subtle but vital distinction, we acknowledge that there is indeed – as H. J. Eysenck described in his 1995 book *Genius*[46] – a higher than normal rate of psychotic illness, a higher than normal rate of psychopathic traits (which include low Agreeableness and low Conscientiousness but also more subtle characteristics)[47] and drug and alcohol problems among geniuses. We would explain this in terms of the Endogenous personality being an evolved adaptation for creativity, but one which is more than usually vulnerable to psychosis, psychopathy and drug addiction when there are further predisposing factors; genetic, environmental, social or whatever. But we regard the genius as being a specialized type

---

[46] Eysenck, H. (1995). *Genius: The Natural History of Creativity.* Cambridge: Cambridge University Press.

[47] According to the American Psychiatric Association the key psychopathic (or Anti-Social Personality Disorder) traits are (1) Inability to sustain consistent work (2) Failure to conform to social norms (3) Irritability and aggressiveness (4) Failure to honour financial obligations (5) Impulsiveness (6) No regard for the truth (7) Recklessness (8) Poor parenting skills (9) Failure to form long-term sexual relationships (due to inability to love) (10) Lack of remorse (11) Conduct Disorder in childhood.

arising as a result of evolution by natural selection; and therefore genius is *not* – as Eysenck tended to think – a result of a partial degree of illness, antisocial personality, sickness or stress.

But the co-occurrence of madness and genius leads to a practical problem when trying to identify genius – how could we discriminate between uncreative insanity and the potential for creative genius? How can one tell if someone has the Endogenous personality type, rather than just being socially-*impaired* for some reason? The difference is real and important.

To do this, we need to examine the Endogenous personality type in more detail. We have seen that there are two main aspects to genius: characteristic personality traits and outlier levels of high intelligence. We will begin with personality traits.

The Endogenous person has a strong inner motivation. He does not avoid groups and social responsibilities simply for negative reasons such as lack of interest, because he wants to do nothing; but because he wants to "do his own thing", because he is powerfully interested in some very specific thing.

The Endogenous person is therefore being *driven* to do something. His mind is usually brooding on his 'problem', full of plans and aims and aspirations. These may or may not come to fruition – some people with an Endogenous personality are late-developers, and may superficially seem to be adrift, or to change direction too frequently to become successful; but they are actually *trying to find their subject*, trying to find their Destiny.

For example; Einstein did not shine at school and failed to achieve his first career aims, doing his first major work and completing a PhD in his spare time while employed as a Patent Office clerk.[48] Francis Crick (1916-2004) attended his second choice university (he was rejected from Cambridge so went to University College, London), achieved only a second class degree, started and gave-up two PhDs, and worked on naval research before he found what he "should" have been doing only in his mid-thirties, going on to co-discover the structure of DNA then making further fundamental contributions to unravelling the genetic code.[49]

Was there anything that could differentiate between drifting potential geniuses who have not yet found their destiny – people like the young Einstein and Crick; and people who are merely-

---

[48] Miller, A. (1999). Albert Einstein. In M. Runco & S. Pritzker (Eds). *Encyclopedia of Creativity*. New York: Academic Press.

[49] Crick, F. (1990). *What Mad Pursuit: A Personal View of Scientific Discovery*. New York: Basic Books; Ridley, Matt (2006). *Francis Crick: Discoverer of the Genetic Code*. Ashland, OH: Atlas Books; Watson, J. D. (1968). *The Double Helix: A Personal Account of the Discovery of the Structure of DNA*. New York: Atheneum.

drifting, starting and failing, unable to apply-themselves because they have something wrong with them?

Extraversion- Introversion trait

What kind of personality results in such a disposition towards genius? We have already looked at the personality type seemingly associated with academics who are regarded as creative in their fields and, indeed, as geniuses in terms of the mainstream 'Big Five' traits.

There are, however, problems in measuring some of these traits when it comes to genius. In general, it would be expected that the genius ought to be high in the Introversion trait – in the sense that introverts are inner-stimulated and autonomous of their environment, in contrast with extraverts who depend on external stimulus to maintain a state of arousal or alertness.

But the self-rating scales for measuring Introversion focus on behaviours and not psychological mechanisms, focus on outcomes not processes – therefore those scoring high in Introversion will include people who are simply anhedonic (unable to experience pleasure), inactive; who lack motivation and drive – and these attributes would be fatal to the prospects of a genius accomplishing anything significant.

In other words, true, underlying Introversion would be a characteristic of genius, but a high score on the Introversion rating scale would also contain under-motivated people – thereby blurring the measurement by misclassification error.

Thus, a genius needs to be a genuine Introvert; but people with various pathologies might lead to "false positive" measures of high Introversion. This may explain the counter-intuitive finding that creative scientists are high in Extraversion – since geniuses are very rare, most of the high Introversion scores are contributed by those suffering from pathology.

Neuroticism – Emotional Stability trait

Analogously, but in the opposite direction, high Neuroticism (N) would be bad for a genius, in the sense that N refers to an unpleasant and overwhelming sensitivity of emotions and moods to the environment – such that a high N person tends easily to be overwhelmed with negative emotions such as anxiety, shyness, low self-esteem, misery etc.

But the opposite state of low-N (or high Emotional Stability) as it is measured by behavioural questionnaires, is also potentially hostile to genius, since it implies an insensitivity to events; a lack of emotional-responsiveness – and low-N-scorers include people with weak emotions and people with emotional insensitivity. These would all tend to be a disadvantage to genius – since emotions are used to evaluate situations and evidence; so weak emotions would tend to impair discrimination.

These would be the underlying processes of Neuroticism, but in practice N is measured using a tally of (usually self-reported) 'superficial' behavioural traits – and these could not distinguish between different causes of the same behaviour; and so would conflate subtle and useful emotional sensitivity, with the pathological state of too-easy triggering of negative emotions.

So, a genius might score as somewhat high in N, simply because he experiences emotions strongly; but this would not necessarily reflect a pathological sensitivity.

Psychoticism – Conscientiousness/ Agreeableness; and Agreeableness/ Empathizing

We have already seen that genius is associated with trait Psychoticism. The inverse correlation of Creativity in terms of Conscientiousness (C) and Agreeableness (A) is understandable, and necessary – once C and A are properly understood.

Creativity implies a strong ego, a person who looks at a situation and comes up with something different because he believes it possible – even probable – that he knows better than other people, and is (to some extent) indifferent to the opinions of others on this matter.

Why does this entail low C? Well, Conscientiousness is sometimes conceptualized in terms of delayed gratification – the ability to put-off gratification now, in return for greater gratification in the future. For example, to defer the pleasure of playing, and instead study academic subjects – foregoing the current pleasure of play, and suffering the tedium of work, for a (hoped for) greater pleasure in the future.

But this is an error – because it is not the way the mind is motivated. The mind actually works by maximizing *current* gratification – by doing what is positively rewarding here and now, and avoiding what yields negative emotions. Therefore, the proper way to conceptualize Conscientiousness is that a high C person gets more gratification here and now by doing what he feels it is best to do, or necessary to do, or which he has been told to do by an authority, or what he is supposed to do according to peer pressure.

Therefore, high C implies a high degree of concern for internalized social norms – a tendency to feel good (here and now) when conforming to these social norms/ values – and/or a tendency to feel bad (e.g. guilty, ashamed, afraid) when transgressing or failing to follow these social norms.

And this is what links Conscientiousness to Agreeableness (or Simon Baron Cohen's trait of Empathizing, which correlates highly with A).[50] High Agreeableness is a self-evaluation for having a dominating concern with the views of other people – paying close attention to knowing the emotions and wishes of others: that is, a calibration of one's own (observed or perceived) behaviours to stay in line with the expectations or desires of others. Such a concern would be fatal to the chances of a genius attaining his Destiny.

So, it can be seen that Conscientiousness and Agreeableness are two sides of the same coin (and the inverse of Psychoticism) – which is that a person high in Conscientiousness and also Agreeableness is one who – here and now, and in the present moment – derives the greatest satisfaction from his conformity to the social group, and is attentive to cues of social group values: and (more important) who has aversive feelings if he

---

[50] Baron-Cohen, S. (2008). *Autism and Asperger Syndrome.* Oxford: Oxford University Press or Baron-Cohen, S. (2004). *The Essential Difference.* London: Penguin. The Endogenous personality can be seen as both low in the female-related trait of Empathizing; and in his non-social, or 'abstract', interests there is a positive and overlapping relationship with Baron Cohen's reciprocal and male-related trait of Systemizing.

transgresses or he fails to follow social norms, such as would happen if creative thinking was in play.

And such a person is *not* creative – because he is focused on learning and doing what the social group wants him to do, instead of what his inner drives tell him he ought to do: needs to do.

Creativity in low Psychoticism people

Although creativity is strongest in those high in the personality trait of Psychoticism (P) when combined with high intelligence (indicating a fundamentally functional and healthy brain), it is not restricted to those of high-P personality: probably, everyone is creative to some extent.

How then does creativity show itself in low-P individuals? – given that the distribution of Psychoticism within the population is 'positively-skewed' – in other words a majority of people are low in Psychoticism, and only a small proportion high in P?

In people low in Psychoticism, creativity is there but weak, seldom activated, not-dominant, short-lived and – as a rule – subordinated to social (including sexual) imperatives which are the primary drive for most people. Of course, almost by definition, creativity in the normal majority of people is not necessarily impressive, and is also rarely activated. So this low-level, relatively-infrequent creativity tends to be private, and almost invisible at a societal level (especially in large modern societies).

The easiest way to see low level creativity is perhaps in children – especially in older but pre-pubertal children (aged about 6-12), and their 'crazes' and hobbies. Boys often have very creative hobbies in which they become mini-experts and avid dissenters on such subjects as cars, aeroplanes, sports, dinosaurs etc. – also in reading (and memorizing) particular books (on favourite themes or by favourite authors), or TV series. These children often live chunks of their leisure time psychologically-inside a very intense parallel 'fantasy world'.

Normal and average creativity is therefore seen in *hobbies*, and how people use their discretionary time; and the fact that hobbies are for most people subordinated to work, relationships and daily life is due to the low-P, low creativity personality.

Normal people are creative, to some subsidiary extent; and they fit creativity into their lives. But geniuses do the opposite: fit their lives around their hobbies; and geniuses usually make their hobbies (their avocations) into their life (their vocations).

The Asocial genius

Humans are social animals: most Men see the world through social spectacles.

But a genius is not like this. The genius does not have a single, stereotypical, positive personality type (because Endogenous personalities are very various in terms of traits such as likeableness, helpfulness, and personal warmth) – but geniuses are characterised by *not* being primarily social animals. A genius is one whose main focus and motivation is not social, nor sexual; but instead abstract, asocial – whether artistic, scientific, technical, or whatever it may be.

Could it then be that the genius uses for abstract thinking, those brain-systems which in most people are used for social intelligence? That in the genius the social intelligence system is wired-up to internal stimuli instead of to social situations? It seems that the genius deploys the social intelligence parts of the brain for other purposes – and that therefore the usual spontaneous motivation and attention that goes to social material is instead – automatically – being harnessed and deployed to deal with other and inner-generated material. This seems to us very likely; although such aspects of brain structure have not yet been reliably measured. But given that the genius brain seems to be hard-wired for both creativity and intelligence; it is plausible that this may be made possible by functional re-deployment of at least some aspects of social/ sexual circuitry.

So, it is not that geniuses lack social intelligence (the genius is not 'autistic' in the sense of having a deficit or defect in social intelligence); rather that geniuses have all the 'equipment' necessary for social intelligence, but are 'wired-up' to use their social intelligence for other and not-social purposes.

Specifically, the genius's social intelligence may be wired-up to internally-generated material (instead of attending to actual people in the environment and from memory). The spontaneous interest and concern with "other people" that is characteristic of most people is, in the genius, directed to whatever 'abstract' subject the genius has a vocation-for.

Another way of thinking about this is that the genius may be able to deploy extra "brain power" in problem solving, by "co-opting" the brain regions normally used for social intelligence. And not only brain power – but the distinctive "theory of mind" mode of thinking which characterises social intelligence. So the genius often thinks about "his subject" in a social-like way – as a world populated by entities with motivations and dispositions and each having a purpose.

Social intelligence could be much of what is creative about creativity; because to think about abstract things 'anthropomorphically' with social intelligence, or animistically as if they were sentient social agents, perhaps opens-up a new and probably more creative, intuitive and flexible way of thinking.[51]

The Endogenous personality also has very high intelligence. This may be apparent through good exam results in a 'g'-loaded evaluation, but may require formal intelligence testing to detect, if the individual has either suffered from poor or absent education, or else lacks the conscientiousness to apply himself to his studies. And sometimes intelligence tests won't do justice to the genius's abilities.

That the intelligence of the Endogenous Personality can sometimes not be identified in a conventional way is of crucial importance. Often, the genius will have extremely pronounced abilities in one area of intelligence – such as verbal intelligence – but will be less skilled in other areas. Einstein, for example, had such high mathematical abilities that he developed an original proof of Pythagoras' theorem at the age of 12. However, his linguistic abilities were so deficient that he failed the entrance exam for the Federal Institute of

---

[51] Charlton, B. G. (2000). *Psychiatry and the Human Condition.* Oxford: Radcliffe.

Technology in Zurich.[52] Consequently, though an IQ test can capture general intelligence it will not necessarily be able to capture genuine genius.

So, the Endogenous personality may be recognized not just by their relative autonomy – that is, their lack of need for social validation and consequent lack of interest in social and sexual matters – but also by their high intelligence and positive motivation to do (or to find) ... whatever it is that they are equipped by their nature to do.

---

[52] Miller, A. (1999). Albert Einstein. In M. Runco & S. Pritzker (Eds). *Encyclopedia of Creativity.* New York: Academic Press.

Chapter Eight

Destiny versus Conscientiousness

The Creative Triad is a minimum requirement, of course, and there are other features that may help to identify a genius. One of the marked features of the Endogenous Personality is a sense of Destiny. This leads to a Quest and, eventually, Illumination. We are prone to think of only the last step in this journey: the *Eureka* moment' of Illumination when the genius is flooded with insight and sees the answer to his problem, and what the answer means. But there are at least three distinct phases of which this comes late.

1. Destiny

From childhood, youth or early adult life there is a sense of destiny, of having some special role to play. This destiny is accepted, not chosen; so that the task is not to manufacture, invent or devise a destiny; but rather to discover, to find-out the nature of one's own personal and unique destiny. Such a process of discovery is a matter of trial and error, following hunches, drifting; false leads, blind alleys and red herrings – there is no recipe for finding one's destiny. Nobody else can do it for you.

2. Quest

After seeking, the genius recognises what it is that he is meant to do (or, meant to attempt): this is his Quest. Now he has to choose – does he embrace his Destiny and accept the Quest? – Or does he refuse? Only he can decide; and he will inevitably decide: the decision is unavoidable.

3. Illumination

After prolonged effort – months, years, a decade or more: *Eureka* moment – Illumination is achieved: the thing is done! (*Eureka* means something like "I have found it!" and is attributed to Archimedes in his bath.)

The experience accumulated, the skills gained, the understanding achieved during the Quest at last come together and the breakthrough is made. A textbook example would be the English architect Michael Ventris (1922-1956). Ventris was plagued by ill-health as a child (he also suffered from night-blindness and extreme short-sightedness) but was blessed with an ability to learn languages. He met the archaeologist Sir Arthur Evans (1851-1941) on a school trip to the Royal Academy in London in 1936, when Ventris was 14. Evans held up some Cretan tablets, written in Linear B script, declaring that nobody could decipher this. Ventris dedicated the rest of his life to cracking Linear B. Ventris finally succeeded in 1952, after which he was reported to lack a sense of purpose. He died in a night time car crash in 1956, aged 34.[53]

Of course there are other phases coming after Illumination – for instance the Illumination must be communicated to others; but beyond a certain minimal effort at recording, reproducing and revealing, effective communication is often 'in the lap of the gods' – and beyond the scope of purposive activities of the genius. Then the Illumination must be understood, considered, implemented, and so on.

The usual life of an Endogenous personality is in stark contrast to that of a Conscientious person, helping us to identify who is closer-to and who is further from genius. The Conscientious personality is driven by external social perceptions – he is attuned to peer pressure, he accepts peer evaluations, and may work hard on problems and jobs which are derived from the social *milieu*.

The Conscientious personality has not chosen his problem; more exactly his problem does not derive from inner sources. He is motivated to act – but by other people, not by trying to solve his own 'problem.' The Conscientious personality has no

---

[53] Robinson, A. (2012). *The Man Who Deciphered Linear B: The Story of Michael Ventris*. London: Thames and Hudson.

sense of being on a track of Destiny; he does not 'own' the problem he is working-on. That line of work may be adopted from obedience, or duty – or as a matter of expediency (e.g. for status, or money, or to get sex). But when a line of work ceases to be externally required, or is externally discouraged, or becomes inexpedient then it will be abandoned.

From this it is clear that the Conscientious personality is not suited to a genius, is un-original and unlikely to lead to breakthroughs. He has the drive to do something in the world; but that something does not derive from within him, and therefore does not mobilize his full inner resources. And his motivation will fail when times are tough – he will not push through discouragements.

In contrast to the externally-orientated Conscientious personality, the Contemplative personality is focused upon the inner world. The mind's eye is turned inward; and the Contemplative personality is meditative; occupied by thoughts, fantasies, speculations ...

However, the contemplative personality is not creative but ... contemplative. For a Contemplative, 'action' is meditative – understanding, experience, the observation of the transcendental such as truth, beauty, virtue, unity... this is what provides the greatest satisfaction.

The Contemplative personality is a dream-er, not a do-er. Therefore, the Contemplative will not summon the long-term, stubborn determination required to do genius-type creative work; the Quest to keep pushing and pushing at a problem until it yields to Illumination – then to communicate the outcome.

The Contemplative personality has the kind of autonomy of 'public opinion' which is necessary to creativity – but lacks motivation towards actions, lacks the 'drive' to solve a problem – instead he is content to contemplate perceived reality rather than to re-conceptualize reality.

Chapter Nine

The Shaman versus the Head Girl

Power, Pre-eminence, Personality

In considering the nature of genius, it is not possible to define it in terms of a single variable – but it requires several factors: the three Ps – 1. Power, 2. Pre-eminence, and 3. Being associated with a Personality.

1. Power

Genius is a form of power. It is indeed a new source of power that adds to human capability. An analogy would be that genius is like discovering a new supply of fuel – a new forest, coal seam or oil field. This new power can be used constructively, or destructively – for tools or for weapons; and a weapon can be used for legitimate defence or for malicious torture.

Genius is somewhat like *a local reorganization of reality* to create new capability or efficiency or effect, the insights and theory necessary for such a reorganization, or a technology or tool that enables such a reorganization.

But if the primary reality of genius is a new source of power, the secondary effect is to redistribute power – specifically to concentrate power around the results of genius (not necessarily around the genius himself, but concentrate power around the product of genius). But it should be noticed that the tendency is for this power to diffuse and disseminate – so that the consequences of genius typically spread much more widely than the situation or society in which the originating genius dwelt.

For example, technologies such as the architectural arch (inventor unknown) spread rapidly and widely across Europe and Asia Minor. The opposite situation, when a breakthrough is confined to the originating group, is rare but does sometimes happen; one example is Greek Fire (inventor unknown) – which was a substance used as a deadly incendiary weapon by the Byzantine Empire, that could continue burning even while floating on water – the secret recipe for which has never been discovered.

2. Pre-eminence

The power of genius is associated with pre-eminence. A genius must also be pre-eminent in his field, must be a person of high ability. Thus, it is not genius when a person is of mediocre ability but merely has power conferred upon him, or has a large effect, but by accident.

3. Personal

Genius is personal; that is, it originates in a specific person. The power and pre-eminence of a genius must also be derived from within themselves, must originate from the person – and not merely from his position in a system or institution or from headship of a team (or from some other person – as when somebody else's work is appropriated).

The Shaman

So, if we want a useful metaphor; the power of the genius is like that of the shaman, in contrast to that of the chief. The power of the genius is like that of German sociologist Max Weber's (1864-1920) 'Charismatic' in contrast to the 'Bureaucrat'[54] who then administers the society which the Charismatic (the one with the gifts to make a cold world seem warm) has founded. The genius may impress her teachers at school, but she is not going to be made Head Girl.

The shaman comparison is, perhaps, the most useful. Now, the category of shaman is a modern, Western conceptualization which unifies disparate figures found in a wide range of tribal situations and

---

[54] See Weber, Max. (1991). The Sociology of Charismatic Authority. In Gerth, H. H. and Mills, C. Wright, (Eds). *From Max Weber: Essays in Sociology.* London: Routledge.

from different historical times. The term was originally Siberian and this may link culturally to Amerindian examples (including among Eskimos/Inuit, through classic 'Red Indians'/ Native Americans; to Amazonians and Patagonians); but shamans are also instanced among the Bushmen of the Kalahari desert in Africa and Aborigines in Australia; and indeed wherever there is an animistic, or simple totemistic (where an animal totem is worshipped and sacrificed) religion. The shaman lives in a world dominated by spirits, everything in the world has its own spirit and that spirit must be appeased through ritual. He has the ability to enter the spirit world, negotiate with the spirits, and so improve the life of the tribe through healing or ensuring good hunting.[55]

As such, despite the many fair points made by revisionists which tend to suggest that the whole area of shamans is so vague and confused that it would be better to dispense with the term; we believe it does have value. The key point is that shamans were unexpected figures for anthropologists – found in some types of simple society; but apparently either completely absent from Western societies – or else hidden so deeply as

---

[55] See, Eliade, M. (2004). *Shamanism: Archaic Techniques of Ecstasy.* Princeton: Princeton University Press; Hutton, R. (2001) *Shamans: Siberian spirituality and the Western imagination.* London: Hambledon.

to be undetectable by official investigators. So anthropologists might have expected to find priests, analogous to the already known priests of the Western, Middle Eastern and Far Eastern societies – but shamans were not priests. A new category was needed.

What do shamans do? They are called upon to deal with exceptional situations – situations where there is no traditional guidance, or where the traditional guidance has been tried and found to be ineffective. Such situations could include some types of illness, when and where to move for better hunting, what to do about threats from predators or other tribes, 'legal' judgement in difficult cases – many types of advice and guidance, interpretation and prophecy.

To do this, shamans use altered states of consciousness – trance states of various types or visionary dreams – during which shamans contact the underlying spirit world for information and prediction, or to intervene and change things. In a nutshell, shamans are believed to be able to come into contact with a deeper level of reality than the everyday – and that is the source of their abilities – and their societal role.

So, shamans are highly creative persons – and therefore we would expect that they would show the Psychoticism-like traits of high creativity; and this seems to be confirmed by anthropological accounts.

Shamans usually emerge from an early age of life – either childhood or teens; the shaman is either marked from an early age as being different, or else goes through a (typically) traumatic experience of illness, accident or some other stress, which changes them permanently. Thus, shamans are seen as flawed, damaged people who also (because of this, not despite it) have special gifts.[56] They are the 'wounded healers' as the Dutch Catholic priest Fr. Henri Nouwen (1932-1996) put it.[57]

The shaman is usually a man – usually not socially integrated, usually lives somewhat apart, may be unfriendly – a person feared and respected rather than loved and cherished. Often the shaman is unmarried, without known children – someone who hands on his social role by apprenticeship rather than founding a lineage. Someone who does not work, but is supported by payments for services and charity/protection money – at least he does not do

---

[56] On shamans, see: Jakobsen, M. (1999). *Shamanism: Traditional and Contemporary Approaches to the Mastery of Spirits and Healing*. Oxford: Berghahn Books; Lewis, I. M. (1989) *Ecstatic Religion: A Study of Shamanism and Spirit Possession*. London: Routledge; Salamone, F. (1995). The Bori and I: Reflections of a Mature Anthropologist. *Anthropology and Humanism*, 20: 15-19.

[57] Nouwen, H. (2013). *The Wounded Healer.* New York: Doubleday.

work as it applies to the rest of the tribe – hunting gathering, agriculture, warfare, child care.[58]

It would obviously help if the shaman was more-than-usually intelligent as well as more-than-usually creative – but it is probable that these nomadic, simple hunter-gatherer societies have not been selected for higher intelligence over hundreds of years – as have some of the more stable and more complex agricultural societies (as we will see later).

So the objective intelligence of real life shamans may have been relatively lower than what Europeans of recent generations would have considered to be average. However, it is likely that shamans were relatively highly intelligent by the standards of their people.

But it is not only the exceptional intelligence that sets the shaman apart – rather it is the different cognitive style: the shaman approaches problems differently, or creatively as we would say – he does not apply the usual, traditional, high status or socially sanctioned rules or practices; but instead generates his unpredictable answers using quite different processes and procedures.

And this is something that the shaman cannot help doing: he is made that way, he is called to a role. The shaman is probably an Endogenous personality; he embodies that power which comes

---

[58] Anthropological accounts of shamans indicate that they are such characters. For example, Salamone, F. Op. cit.

from high ability combined with high creativity, and it is this which enables him to serve a crucial social function in certain rare but important situations. Most of the time he is not wanted, scary, chaotic, nasty, a nuisance, a parasite – but there are situations when he is needed. And it is for these situations that the shaman is protected by the rest of the tribe.

This, then, is the same kind of power the genius has: the shaman can be considered an example of the 'local genius'.

The Head Girl

As already mentioned, a comparison, or anti-comparison, with genius is the 'Head Girl.'

The first issue is simply this word 'Girl.' Genius tends to more common in males. There are a number of reasons for this:

1. Women's intelligence is more bunched towards the mean than male intelligence, meaning there are more intelligence outliers among men.
2. Adult men probably have a moderately higher average IQ score than women (perhaps one third of a standard deviation higher) – which (like the wider standard deviation of male IQ) also trans-

lates to a more substantial proportion of men at the very highest levels of intelligence.[59]

3. In surveys, men are nearly always rated higher than women in average Psychoticism; and people with high levels of Psychoticism are much more likely to be men than women (the distribution of Psychoticism is positively-skewed in most studies – that is most people have low levels of P, and only a small proportion have high levels). We would interpret this sex difference as partly being due to higher rates of psychopathy/ 'psychopathic personality disorder' in men; but partly also an aspect of the more creative, Endogenous, personality type.[60]

It is noticeable that girls' crazes tend to be more socially-inflected and less abstract (e.g. princesses, fairies, clothes, ponies); and this follows through to adult life, and to the subjects of major achievement for women. The highest frequency of genius-level, or near-genius level, achievement among women is focused on the most social and human aspects of the arts and sciences – and much rarer in abstract areas. For instance, there are many and well known women novelists in the front rank (notably Jane

[59] Lynn, R. & Irwing, P. (2004). Sex differences on the Progressive Matrices: A meta-analysis. *Intelligence,* 32: 481-498.
[60] Eysenck, H. J. (1992). The definition and measurement of Psychoticism. *Personality and Individual Differences*, 13: 757-785; Dutton (2014), Op. cit., Ch. 11.

Austen and George Eliot) – the novel being the most 'social' of art forms. And in science, the highest achievements of women are in the human sciences rather than the physical sciences – and within biology women have been very prominent in social areas like primatology (e.g. Jane Goodall, Sarah Blaffer Hrdy) and anthropology (e.g. Ruth Benedict, Jane Jacobs).

It is a tenet of feminist 'scholarship' that there were many women geniuses who were neglected because they were women; and a large part of feminist scholarship has been dedicated to raising awareness of women geniuses. That there are indeed women geniuses is clear – examples abound, especially in literature; but we do not think feminist scholarship of the past fifty years has come up with a single 'neglected' example of a major woman genius.

Instead there has been a combination of the pretence that real women geniuses were 'previously neglected' until feminism came along; plus the hyping of women non-geniuses (such as Hildegard of Bingen as a composer and spiritual writer, the DNA scientist Rosalind Franklin, and playwright Aphra Benn). But Feminist scholarship has failed to discover any real women geniuses, because there have been relatively few.

The 'Head Girl' is thus even more problematic in terms of genius. The stereotypical Head Girl is an all-rounder: performs extremely well in all school subjects and has a very high 'Grade Point Average' as it is termed in the USA. She is excellent at sports, Captaining all the major teams. She is also pretty, popular, sociable and well-behaved.

The Head Girl will probably be a big success in life, in whatever terms being a big success happens to be framed (she will gravitate towards such aspects of life) – so she might in some times and places make a good marriage and do a great job of raising a family; in another time and place she might go to a top-notch college and get a top-notch job – and pursue a glamorous and infertile lifestyle of 'serial monogamy'; with desirable mates.

But the Head Girl is not, cannot be, a creative genius. The genius is pretty much everything the Head Girl is not. He (or she) is lop-sided in his abilities – truly excellent at some things or maybe just one thing, he is either hopeless or bored by many others. He won't work hard for long periods at things he does not want to do. He will not gravitate to the prestige areas of life and cannot, or will not, do the networking necessary to get-on.

The Head Girl can never be a creative genius because she does what other people want by the standards they most value. She will work harder and at a higher standard in doing whatever it is that social pressure tells her to do – and she will do this by whatever social standards prevail, only more thoroughly. Meanwhile the creative genius will do what he does because he must.

The Head Girl will not want to alienate potentially powerful allies. Meanwhile the creative genius is indifferent or hostile to the opinions of others so long as he knows he is right.

The Head Girl is great to have around, everybody thinks she is wonderful. Meanwhile the creative genius is at best a person who divides opinion, strongly, in both directions – at worst often a signed-up member of the awkward squad.

The vulnerable genius

The proper social role of the highly able Endogenous personality is not as leader. Indeed, the Endogenous personality should be excluded from leadership as he will tend to lack the desire to cooperate with or care for the feelings of others. His role should be as an intuitive/ inspired 'adviser' of rulers.

Adviser-of-rulers is a term which should be taken to include various types of prophet, shaman, genius, wizard, hermit, and holy fool – the Socrates of the early Platonic dialogues is an historical example, as is Diogenes, the Cynic, of Sinope (c.412-323 BC), who lived in a barrel and is supposed to have snubbed Alexander the Great (without being punished), or even the Fool character in Shakespeare plays.

These are extremes; but the description of Endogenous personality and of an 'inner orientation' also applies to most historical examples of creative genius. The Endogenous personality – therefore – does not (as most men) seek primarily for social, sexual or economic success; instead the Endogenous personality wants to live by his inner imperatives.

The way it is supposed-to-work, the 'deal', the 'social contract'; is that the Endogenous personality, by his non-social orientation, is working for the benefit of society as a whole; at the cost of his not competing in the usual status competitions within that society. His 'reward' is simply to be allowed, or – better – actively enabled, to have the minimal necessary sustenance, psychological support (principally being 'left alone' and not harassed or molested; but ideally sustained by his family, spouse, patron or the like) to be somehow provided-with the time and space and wherewithal to do his work and communicate the outcome. For the Endogenous personality, this is its own reward.

In return, the Endogenous personality should not expect (although he might, by chance, get) social esteem, wealth, or sexual success. Often, he may need to be highly solitary, secluded, ascetic, perhaps celibate. He should not seek, and should try not to accept, leadership positions, or administrative responsibilities.

Michael A. Woodley makes the point that individuals who can properly be classified as geniuses necessarily have brains that are wired differently from normal; they are programmed to focus on their destined tasks and therefore may be unable to deal with the small details of day to day affairs.[61] For instance, Einstein once got lost not far from his home in Princeton, New Jersey. He went into a shop and said, 'Hi, I'm Einstein, can you take me home please?' He could not drive a car, and many tasks and chores that most people take for granted were beyond him.[62]

Woodley's conclusion flows from the idea of genius as a group-selected trait adapted to be an asset to other people. In sum, the potential genius needs to be looked after; because in terms of negotiating the complexities of human society he is likely to be vulnerable and fragile. The corollary of which is that when geniuses are *not* looked after, they are less likely to fulfil their potential, and everybody loses.

---

[61] Quoted in Kealey, H. (14 November 2014). Why do geniuses lack common sense? *Daily Telegraph,* http://www.telegraph.co.uk/news/science/11232300/Why-do-geniuses-lack-common-sense.html (Accessed 13 August 2015).

[62] Hoffmann, B. (1972). *Albert Einstein: Creator and Rebel.* London: Hart-Davis.

For instance, the American reclusive poet Emily Dickinson (1830-1886) was 'managed' by Colonel T.W. Higginson; Jane Austen (1775-1817) flourished in the obscurity of her family and the critic and social philosopher John Ruskin (1819-1900) was sheltered and nurtured by his parents, then a cousin. Thomas Aquinas (1225-1274) was looked after by his brother Friars; Genetics-founder Johann Mendel (1822-1884) was secluded in a monastery; Pascal (1623-1662) was looked after by his aristocratic French family.[63] Plus many another genius was sustained by a capable wife – Kurt Gödel (1906-1978) depended on his, older, wife Adele; and would only eat food prepared by her; so that when she was hospitalized, Gödel literally starved.[64]

When there is a close-knit and idealistic community, this may also do it – for example, the community of mathematicians looked after

[63] See: Kirk, C. (2004). *Emily Dickinson: A Biography*. Bolder: Greenwood; Tucker, G. (1995). *Jane Austen, the Woman: Some Biographical Insights.* London: Palgrave MacMillan; Copleston, F. (1991). *Aquinas: An Introduction to the Life and Work of the Great Medieval Thinker.* London: Penguin; Henig, R. (2001). *The Monk in the Garden: The Lost and Found Genius of Gregor Mendel, the Father of Genetics.* Houghton, Mifflin, Harcourt; O'Connell, M. (1997). *Blaise Pascal: Reasons of the Heart.* Grand Rapids: Wm. B. Eerdmans.
[64] Wang, H. (1987). *Reflections on Kurt Gödel*. MIT Press, p.15.

Hungarian Paul Erdos (1913-1996), who never had a home, possessed only the contents of a small suitcase, and camped-out at in the house of one mathematics professor after another for decades, while collaborating on research papers. The Indian genius mathematician Srinivasa Ramanujan (1887-1920) was discovered and protected by the Cambridge Professors Hardy and Littlewood – although he died, weakened by his inability to eat adequately due to Brahmin dietary restrictions that were too rigorous for English life.

The unfortunate William Sidis (1898-1944), an American child prodigy of the early twentieth century and reputed to have the highest ever recorded IQ score; was exploited and exposed to social stresses rather than protected by his parents (his father was a Harvard professor of Psychology). Sidis was a sensitive and awkward man who had to survive in a hostile and mocking world; so his creative achievements – although greater than commonly supposed – were limited, and indeed largely unknown and unappreciated.[65]

---

[65] See: Hoffman, P. (1999). *The Man Who Only Loved Numbers: The Story of Paul Erdos and the Search for Mathematical Truth*. Hyperion Books; Kanigel, R. (1991). *The Man Who Knew Infinity: A Life of the Genius Ramanujan*. Hachette; Wallace, A. (1986). *The Prodigy: A Biography of William Sidis, the World's Greatest Child Prodigy*. London: MacMillan.

The Rise of Bureaucracy

Modern society is dominated by 'bureaucracy', that is by division of function, voting committees and formal procedures – rather than by individual humans, close-knit and informal groups making personal judgments.

This impersonality of bureaucracy, the lack of individual autonomy and responsibility; seems to be a major factor in the modern failure to look-after, but instead to neglect or even to persecute, geniuses.

Furthermore, in itself, the rise in bureaucracy – in academia and also more broadly – might be seen as further evidence of the trend for decline in intelligence. There are a number of complementary explanations for the rise in bureaucracy which would be congruent with this theory.

1. Parasitism: Bureaucracy can be seen as a parasite, growing at the expense of the host society. Some bureaucracy is necessary as society becomes more complex and organizations become larger. However, the abundance of wealth and resources created by industrialization has meant that it is possible for a group of quite unnecessary people – e.g. micro-managing and inefficiency-generating bureaucrats – to latch onto the host and even persuade the host that they are necessary. Once attached to the host they spread like a cancer

115

because criticism of bureaucracy leads to further 'regulatory' bureaucracy to sort-out the bureaucracy. A more intelligent host would realise that the bureaucracy was parasitic and would remove it – but once the bureaucracy is large enough, then it will dominate all senior positions and committees, and become impossible to excise. At that point, death of the host – along with the parasite – becomes almost inevitable. [66]

2. Division of Labour: Bureaucracy tends to involve an increasing division of labour and the assumption that the decision of a committee will be superior to the (potentially corrupt) decision of an individual. Such division and oversight functions would be more necessary in a society with declining intelligence, because individual decisions would be more prone to corruption and plain stupidity than in a more intelligent society; and people in general would be less likely to trust individuals as intelligence predicts trust.[67] Accordingly, in the context of universities, for example, there would increasingly be a need for more rigid and impersonal personnel selection in the form of

---

[66] See Charlton, B. G. (2010). The cancer of bureaucracy: How it will destroy science, medicine, education; and eventually everything else. *Medical Hypotheses,* 74: 961-965.

[67] Sturgis, P., Read, S., & Allum, N. (2010). Does intelligence foster generalized trust? An empirical test using the UK birth cohort studies. *Intelligence*, 38, 45–54.

requiring formal qualifications achieved *via* rigid criteria. In addition, bureaucracy includes breaking up a task into smaller component functions coordinated in a hierarchical sequence. It takes less intelligence to perform these smaller functions than the entire specialised task. Thus, as society becomes less intelligent so greater bureaucracy is required for even necessary bureaucracy to continue (or for parasitic bureaucracy to continue to grow).

3. The Growth of Academia. As society has become specialised, academia has grown enormously; initially from social need, later from the parasitic growth of functionally redundant and ineffective demands for certification – sustained by increasing state subsidies. As the academic staffing of ever-more institutions expands many-fold, the intellig-ence range of academics is likely to become far broader than it once was, and the tail of less able academics comes to dominate numerically. In addition, the population trend of declining intelligence will mean that even the best academics will be less intelligent than a generation ago. As such, a larger and more effective bureaucracy apparently becomes more necessary (or, at least, desirable) to police and manage a less intelligent (and less self-motivated) academia; which is likely to be increasingly corrupt, incompetent and factious. In addition, we have seen that intelligence correlates with 'Intellect', and universities have become far less intellectual. Instead of acting primarily as a specialist intellectual 'finishing school', they train people – either partially or completely – for various professions: solicitor, engineer, school teacher, government administrator, private industry managers of many types, architect, accountant etc. Until as recently as the 1970s, none of these required a degree – now they do; as do a multitude of skilled manual jobs like pharmacy, physiotherapy, nursing etc. This can be seen to herald a change in attitude. Universities were primarily about training professionals which were originally priests, barristers and physicians only – but the notion of 'profession' has been expanded a hundredfold; and now a university degree is a pre-requisite for even reasonably-paid jobs – unrelated to the actual needs of those jobs. This will select for students who are better at attaining qualifications, at working in a bureaucracy; hence the selection procedures favour those who are Conscientious rather than geniuses.

4. *The Only Means of Achievement.* We have seen that academic achievement is partly predicted by intelligence and partly predicted by personality traits, especially Conscientiousness, which predicts

years spent in education at 0.55.[68] Accordingly, in principle, someone can get into a good university *via* 1. The combination of very high intelligence but only moderate Conscientiousness, 2. Very high Conscientiousness but only moderate intelligence or 3. By scoring reasonably highly on both measures. Bureaucracy – the keeping of records, planning, and adherence to formal procedures (the qualities of a Conscientious person in many ways) – should be smaller, at any given stage of complexity, the more intelligent (on average) is a given society. This is because intelligence reflects a high functioning brain and thus superior memory (swifter learning and less need to record things), superior ability to solve any given problem (and so less need for formal procedures and planning), and being more functionally pro-social and more forward-thinking (meaning less conflict, less free-riding, more trust, and fewer unforeseen problems to manage). Thus, as society becomes less intelligent it can only maintain its achievement level through more Conscientious behaviour: that is, through more bureaucracy.

But, whatever is behind the growth in bureaucracy, whatever mixture of need and

---

[68] Almlund, M., Duckworth, A., Heckman, J. & Kautz, T. (2011). Personality, psychology and economics. In S. Hanushek, S. Machin & L. Woesmann (Eds). *Handbook of the Economics of Education,* Amsterdam: Elsevier.

parasitism that might prevail in any particular time and place, it leads to decision by committees of bureaucrats who will implicitly be looking for people who will make good bureaucrats and often who will make a university money in the relatively short term. They will not want people who will upset the smooth functioning of the bureaucracy – which genius types may well do – and they will be rigid in sticking to rules, which geniuses won't be. It will also be very difficult to punish bureaucrats in voting committees for making a poor decision – for instance, rejecting a person who later turns-out to be a genius in the field, and whose appointment would therefore have eventually paid-off – as rejection was a collective decision where they merely followed the rules; also the composition of the decision-making committee is (typically) unstable and constantly changing. Moreover, bureaucratic "sticking to the rules" will typically work against geniuses, because bureaucrats usually have a black-and-white interest in qualifications, grades and the like. This will be problematic for the genius, with his highly narrow, lop-sided focus. (We have noted elsewhere that Newton, Einstein, Crick and many another genius did not excel academically by formal criteria).

In sum, committees do not look after geniuses – rather they ignore them, or persecute them. It is likely no coincidence that English genius very suddenly all-but disappeared in the era from about 1955-1980[69] in which bureaucracy waxed dominant in national life – and nowadays geniuses are absent, invisible, or fighting for survival against the forces of mass media, committees, peer reviewers and other faceless officials.

This is sad for the geniuses; perhaps fatal for our society.

---

[69] This is discussed in more detail in, Charlton, B.G., & Andras, P. (2005). Medical research funding may have over-expanded and be due for collapse. *QJM*, 98: 53-5; Charlton, B.G. (2009) Why are modern scientists so dull? How science selects for perseverance and sociability at the expense of intelligence and creativity, *Medical Hypotheses*. 72: 237-243.

Chapter Ten

Newton versus Jung

To further illustrate the nature of genius, it will be useful to explore two examples. The first is Sir Isaac Newton (1642-1727); a genius, and one of the very greatest.[70] The second is Carl Jung (1875-1961), who displayed aspects of genius; perhaps a highly influential partial genius.[71]

Newton's intellectual ability, his intelligence, was very obviously stratospheric; so his personality becomes a source of fascination. Hans Eysenck established that the high level creative personality type was approximated by the trait of High Psychoticism, which we have already discussed.

Newton's biography reveals that he was an extreme example of the Psychoticism trait. Psychoticism is important to genius because it describes someone who is uninterested and uninfluenced by the normal human concerns – which are essentially 'other people.' Most humans are social animals, who see life through social spectacles, and who are motivated by the desire for

---

[70] For a full biography of Newton see, Westfall, R. (1983). *Never At Rest: A Biography of Isaac Newton.* Cambridge: Cambridge University Press.
[71] On Jung, see, Blair, D. (2003). *Jung.* New York: Little Brown & Co.

friends, sex, status, and so on. But not Newton. In his early and most creative years, he simply wanted to be allowed to get on with his work.

As a child and young man of science he would spend nearly all of his time alone, when in company he would be silent, he had essentially no friends, formed no relationships with women, and made very little effort to fit-in. Indeed as a boy his relationships with other boys tended to be antagonistic and at times rather sadistic (Newton was not likeable).

Newton was taught Latin at school; and little else. In terms of mathematics and science he was an autodidact. Whatever he did, he did because he wanted to do it; and he did it at close to 100 per cent effort. Thus in a year or so he went from knowing no mathematics to mastering the subject and being among the best in the world; and then immediately went on to make some of the greatest ever mathematical discoveries.

Newton's own explanation of his achievement emphasized the distinctive creative personality – he was asked how he made his discoveries and gave such answers as 'By thinking on it continually' and 'I keep the subject constantly before me'.

Then he all-but dropped mathematics, and instead worked on one area of physics after another – making major discoveries, then moving-on. This may remind you of the 'schoolboy crazes' or obsessions, typical of some highly intelligent young men.

Stories of Newton's consuming focus abound – he would think solidly for hour upon hour – sometimes standing lost in abstraction half way down the stairs; forget to eat, forget to sleep; forget that he had visitors. For years he seldom left his college, almost never left Cambridge. In all of human history there can have been very few (and perhaps nobody of Newton's astonishing intelligence) who gave such intense and sustained concentration to whatever problem they were working on.

And while Newton's academic performance was good, it was not amazing, and was somewhat erratic. It seems he performed badly in his BA examination – which was a *viva voce* disputation; needing to go on to a second round of questions (rather than passing straight away). This was regarded as somewhat disgraceful.

His methods were highly intuitive, reasoning from a relatively small base of axioms and principles, building out from them, making predictions and testing his ideas against general observations. This can be contrasted with the method typical of highly intelligent and conscientious *un*-creative people – who read widely, learn many facts, and then try to apply other-people's solutions to problems.

But Newton, the autodidact, worked things through for himself; thought things through using only those facts and principles he trusted. From this; originality follows quite naturally and without being deliberately sought.

It is clear that Newton's solitary, wilful and autonomous personality; his un-empathic, un-conscientious, anti-social and eccentric ways – in sum his high Psychoticism traits – were as necessary a part of his supreme genius as was ultra-high intelligence.

Let us now contrast Newton with Jung. Carl Jung is unusual among probable-geniuses, in that he was dishonest about his own work and its implications.

That Jung was a near-genius we think is correct; he made numerous discoveries and conceptual breakthroughs – and he is an unseen but pervasive influence behind vast areas of modern culture including psychology, psychiatry, therapy and (especially) that vast and vague phenomenon called the New Age movement (almost everything about the New Age has a Jungian lineage – even when this is not generally known or acknowledged).

But that Jung was a thoroughly-dishonest and deceptive man is something equally undeniable. Jung was never plain and honest when that was inexpedient – Jung was not driven by a pure pursuit of truth; because truth was readily and repeatedly sacrificed when the consequences were unwanted by Jung. (Eysenck regarded lying as typical of the high Psychoticism personality.)

He craved respectability as a Professor, psychiatrist, scholar, scientist – and would trim his published views to ensure this. He wanted wealth, status, admiration – and patients were charmed, seduced, strung-along and generally exploited to ensure this. Jung wanted to be regarded as an unworldly sage – but worked to create an organization dedicated to his own self-promotion. He apparently had many sexual relationships with his patients and trainees right into old age; and had a long-term live-in mistress who functioned as a second wife (while being unmentioned in his autobiography – he also used his personal magnetism to maintain a household of handmaidens to dote upon and serve him).

The point is that Jung's many compromises, deceptions, evasions, and lies are so consistently dedicated to his own comfort, convenience and gratification that the picture is one of a highly charming and dominant; but heartless, manipulative and selfish psychopath – typical traits of high Psychoticism, but which interfere with creative achievement. Furthermore, Jung experienced a significant psychotic episode (his 'confrontation with the unconscious, from 1913) characterized by hallucinations and probably delusions.

In sum, Jung – like Newton – exhibited some aspects of the dark side of Psychoticism.

Jung is, in several respects, the precursor of the postmodern intellectual – the 'clever silly' who espouses an illogical, incoherent, dogmatic, opaquely expressed, and overly complex idea. Doing this helps him to display his intelligence – because the idea is complex and hard to understand, making him seem profound to silly or emotional people – even if the idea is nonsense on closer inspection. Also, if the idea gives people hope, then he will come across as altruistic, further boosting his status.[72]

But this could be put aside as mere hypocrisy – and that is something of which we are all guilty (it would be hypocritical to pretend otherwise). But Jung's dishonesty went even deeper than that, to invade his primary achievement. Because Jung's work is incoherent at the very deepest level – and this incoherence has afflicted his legacy. And this incoherence was not the result of confusion, but the result of dishonesty.

An example is the idea of synchronicity; which has become an extremely influential cultural idea,

---

[72] See Dutton and van der Linden (2015), Op. cit. The original 'clever silly' model – developed by Dutton and van der Linden – was presented in Charlton, B. G. (2009). Clever sillies: Why high IQ people tend to be deficient in common sense. *Medical Hypotheses,* 73: 867-870.

as a buzz-word and a vague concept – but which was deployed by Jung in a way that makes no sense. And this incoherence is not due to misunderstanding Jung, but comes directly from Jung's written contradictory accounts and evasions of the implications of his own insight.

British philosopher Colin Wilson (1931-2013) exposed this in his marvellously insightful short study: *Lord of the Underworld: Jung and the Twentieth Century* (1984); especially the chapter "The Sage of Kusnacht", where Wilson goes through the writings on synchronicity with a fine-toothed comb, and tries to pin down what Jung really believed, or meant – and comes up against a mass of obfuscation and self-refutation: of giving with one hand and taking back with the other.[73]

This kind of contradiction and vagueness vitiates Jung's legacy and is a direct consequence of his mixed motivations. It demonstrates that genius depends on dedication to the work, and any failures in this regard will detract from the level of achievement.

Jung's last recorded words from his death bed seem appropriate: 'Let's have a really good red wine tonight.' The final statement of a man whose personal gifts were astonishingly great – but who

---

[73] Wilson, C. (1984). *Lord of the Underworld: Jung and the Twentieth Century*. Wellingborough: Aquarian Press.

consistently and successfully deployed them for his own comfort, convenience and glory.

Chapter Eleven

The Evolution of Genius

But how did human societies evolve such that genius – which is at least a-social and perhaps seems anti-social, and often indifferent to reproduction – could manifest itself? On the face of it, genius seems like something that could not happen.

In biological, that is evolutionary, terms – and following-up the insights of Michael A. Woodley; we regard genius is an *altruistic* trait.

Altruistic in this sense means that – on average, in the environment where and when genius evolved – being a genius will tend to reduce the genius's own personal reproductive success, while genius-caused inventions and other breakthroughs will usually substantially enhance the reproductive success of the group of which the genius is a member. But this genius-caused enhancement of group survival and growth includes unrelated group members, and group members who have not helped the genius – meaning that kin selection and mutual assistance/ reciprocity (the main posited evolutionary causes of altruism) do not seem to apply.

That is, being a genius on average *reduces* the chances of reproducing successfully, and reduces the probable number of viable children – but the activities of a genius will tend to increase chances of survival of his group, or expand the numbers of people in the group.

Many geniuses have had no known offspring, and statistical studies have indicated a considerably lower-than-average number of children for the geniuses of history.[74] And however imprecise or subjective these studies may be: certainly there is no significant evidence to suggest that geniuses have on average an increased number of offspring – which would be needed to explain the occurrence of genius by ordinary, individual-level selection.

Thus, in terms of survival and reproduction, *being a genius is bad for the genius and good for his group*.

Biological altruism does not (or does not necessarily) correspond with social altruism, or an altruistic personality- i.e. 'helping people' – because the genius's contribution to his community is *via* his work.

Indeed, it is characteristic of the behaviour of a genius that he will protect the conditions necessary for his work, even when this goes against usual and

---

[74] For a discussion of the tendency for geniuses to be celibate and childless see: Simonton, D. K. (2003). Exceptional creativity across the life span: The emergence and manifestation of creative genius. In L.V. Shavina (Ed.), *The International Handbook of Innovation* (pp. 293-308). New York: Pergamon Press.

expected socially altruistic behaviour. The genius may therefore be solitary – may indeed be selfish, may not marry or have a family, may not be a good neighbour. But he is selfish not really for his own benefit – not for money or status – but primarily for the work: selfish to enable him better to do (or to do at all) what it is that he does. He is selfish in pursuit of his Destiny, and that Destiny is for the benefit of others.

Some geniuses are nice, many are nasty – but that is not the point. The point is that the genius feels his first (or a very high) responsibility is to do his utmost to create and sustain the best conditions he needs for his work, and to do that work, and communicate that work. He feels his duty is to follow his Destiny. And this motivation comes above the desire to help other people.

(If asked, a genius might truthfully claim to be working for the long-term benefit of his general group – even when this was at the cost of failing to be helpful here and now, in the immediate- and short-term; to his immediate family, friends and colleagues.)

Thus it is quite possible, indeed it is quite normal, for biological altruism at the group level to go with personal selfishness; and for personal un-selfishness to be anti-altruistic, and to damage the reproductive interests of the group. Dean Simonton has found that many geniuses – most obviously

Newton, but also many others such as Einstein – were extremely difficult people.[75] By contrast, one can imagine a selfless and kindly person who might assist an individual, out of utter kindness, who was part of a group that was effectively at war with the group of which she was a part. Altruism and being nice: two very different things.

The Paradox of the Endogenous personality is that despite their relative indifference to socio-sexual imperatives; we believe that geniuses have (in evolutionary terms) evolved to serve the group.

The Paradox is that only an inner-orientated personality can be sufficiently independent of the social consensus so as to be able to change the social consensus – when that is needed.

Group selection of the Endogenous personality.

In effect, and on average, the Endogenous personality sacrifices his own differential reproductive success – including his inclusive fitness, that is, the reproductive success of his closer kin – to favour the reproductive success of the group. By this group, we usually mean the genius's ethnic or local group.

Australian biologist Frank Salter's detailed mathematical modelling based on population genetic data has shown that, although there is a

---

[75] Simonton (1988), Op. cit.

social dimension to ethnic identification, the core of ethnic group membership is genetic. Ethnic groups are breeding populations, and a random member of one ethnic group will have more genetically in common with a random co-ethnic than he will with a random member of another ethnic group. As such, there are two ways to pass one one's genes: directly (through having children) or indirectly (by abetting one's kin in having children).[76]

This is called inclusive fitness or kin selection – and it means that what looks like altruism at the individual level may be selfishness at the genetic level – indeed, individual altruism is what makes possible genetic selfishness. It works in such a way that the closer the relationship of those who are benefitted, the more powerful is this mechanism – so kin selection is the presumed mechanism that generates the close cooperation and self-sacrifice of social insects such as bees and ants, and most aspects of the 'clannishness' of families and closely-genetically-related humans.

A further theoretically possible mechanism for kin selection would be when an individual does not himself reproduce but substantially assists the reproduction of his genetic relatives, as might happen if an uncle without children gave a lot of

---

[76] Salter, F. (2006). *On Genetic Interests: Family, Ethnicity and Humanity in an Age of Mass Migration.* New Brunswick, NJ: Transaction Publishers.

help to his nieces and nephews, and thereby indirectly promoted the reproduction of the genes he shares with his brother or sister. However, there is no evidence to suggest that geniuses help their genetic relatives any more than non-geniuses, and indeed the genius is likely to do *less* (not more) than average to assist his family – given that he is so devoted to his destined work and problem-solving or otherwise creative activities.

But group selection may be less direct than this; because genius is enhancing the reproductive success of the whole group in a way that typically benefits those who are only distantly related, to the genius – as much or more than the work of a genius benefits close genetic relations (and the family of the genius may also be losing resources by helping to support him).

The ethnic group is merely a highly extended kin network and the genius has no interest in sex or even kindness to his near kin, it would make sense that his evolutionary strategy would favour more distant kin. The group are – in broad terms – an extended family; and the growth of the group may indeed favour the kin of the genius – but this expansion would not necessarily benefit close kin more than remote relations – and the close kin typically have to bear the costs of supporting the genius .

So if we assume that the genius is an evolved adaptation for the good of the group; then what function does the Endogenous personality perform? In a nutshell, *we suggest that the function of the genius is to solve problems which arise from inter-group conflict* – and the benefits a genius provides are typically shared among the whole group among whom he dwells.

Just as the normal situation of individual selection arises from conflict between individuals, so the less common situation of group selection arises from competition between groups – especially when the group is cohesive and the reproductive success of individuals depends upon the survival and expansion of the group.

(Note: There is not, at present, a general and accepted mechanism to explain many or most instances of group selection – although there are some specific suggestions for specific situations. We are therefore arguing that group selection is primarily responsible for evolving the Endogenous personality – but we make no general claims here about how exactly this group selection is operating, at a mechanistic or process level.)

Group conflict and group selection

Group conflict includes situations in which the individual is dependent on the group, and when the group is under extreme pressure from the 'environment.' This is a situation in which only the group *as a group* (and not individuals nor extended families), can survive in a harsh environment, especially in competition with other groups in a similar situation.

The 'environment' includes both natural and social environments. Natural environmental pressure could be extreme temperatures (hot or cold), marked seasonality of food availability, or predation from large animals when these problems can only be solved by the group (e.g. the clan or tribe) cooperating and working together, and cannot be solved by individuals or families pursuing their own specific genetic interests. Social environmental pressure could include group versus group conflicts ('warfare') driven by factors like competition for land or other finite resources.

In the face of a potentially fatal social problem an individual with the Endogenous personality offers the possibility (but of course there is no *guarantee*) of a novel 'breakthrough' answer. For instance, in the face of the prospect of annihilation by the environment, or by another group – a situation in which the group is doomed *unless* there is a breakthrough; perhaps some new technology, some socially-unifying art or form of religion, some way of extracting more resources per unit area, some new weapon or defence. For this kind of *creative solution*, a genius is needed.

If a whole society was composed of genius-type people, it could not function – indeed it would not be a society. But if it altogether lacked Endogenous personalities, then it would only grow very slowly (perhaps by incremental trial and error – which doesn't always yield an answer to novel problems) and would be at greater risk of being wiped-out by natural forces or group competition.

Thus, we can conceive of roughly two kinds of genius. The scientific-technical genius will increase the chances of a sci-tech breakthrough, or a novel theory that will lead to these. For example, inventions such as the spade, bow and arrow, wheel, plough, railway, radio... these are assumed to be products of sci-tech geniuses; and their value is obvious. This kind of genius may help either group survival or even help to expand the group of which he is part.

By contrast, an artistic, philosophical or religious genius will implicitly aid group cohesion – we term these *cohesion geniuses*. Improved cohesion could therefore be the explanation for the occurrence of artistic genius, or the genius of a storyteller – and also an explanation for religious geniuses who invent new interpretations, beliefs, practices, rituals, stories, scriptures, priesthoods or other forms of institution... that have the consequence of binding-together the group.

Improved cohesion from a religious innovation might then help to enhance growth of the group of religious adherents, perhaps the growth of new forms of political organization, and these might result in the increase of (for example) economic activity or military prowess.

Consider the difference between the Kalahari Bushmen in Africa, and Australian Aborigines. These are broadly similar hunter gatherer societies with a similar level of technology and a similar type of environment. The main social difference is in group size – the Aborigines have significantly larger groups, which means that they cohere better and could assemble larger fighting forces. And the larger Aborigine groups are based around their Totemic religion, which is more fixed and more complex than the fluid, imprecise Animism of the Kalahari Bushmen. Animism is the belief that all living things have souls or spirits and these need to be appeased. Totemism develops this belief, and involves the view that there is one primary source in nature which provides the basis of human life in one's tribe. The tribe then tends towards worshipping this specific animal – or whatever it may be – to a greater extent than others. Indeed, regular rituals bring the tribe together as they sacrifice the animal in question.[77]

The Aborigine religion both requires and benefits from a more elaborate social structure of authority and learning of the legends – which must be transmitted through the generations by songs and chants. Presumably (of course there is no direct evidence) some (or more than one) Aborigine religious genius created this Totemic social structure – and the group who adopted it was rewarded by improved cohesion, which enabled them to out-grow and displace rival groups[78].

This is conjectural, albeit plausible – it may or may not be historically true; but our point is that somebody at some time made these religious innovations and enabled larger scale and more powerful social cohesion – and this person could be termed a genius (albeit on a local scale) And perhaps many other examples of genius could be regarded as making creative breakthroughs of a cohesion-generating type.

---

[77] See Lee, R., Daly, R. (Eds) (1999) *Cambridge Encyclopedia of Hunters and Gatherers.* Cambridge: Cambridge University Press; Harvey, G. (2013). *Animism: Respecting the Living World.* Columbia University Press.

[78] See: Howells, W. (2005). *An Introduction to Aboriginal Studies.* Cengage Learning Australia, p.80, and Guenther, M. (1999). *Tricksters and Trancers: Bushman Religion and Society.* Indiana University Press, p.231.

More obvious are the motivational and organizational 'cohesion geniuses' who expand the geographical territory of their group – the geniuses of military defence or conquest; the likes of Alexander the Great, Julius Caesar, Admiral Lord Nelson.

We would also expect different populations to produce differing levels of genius, due to differences in local and regional environments. This is something that has been highlighted by Charles Murray in his book, *Human Accomplishment.*[79]

Murray finds that Europeans are behind the overwhelming majority of important scientific and artistic accomplishments between Classical times and 1950. Northeast Asians are in second place, but their contribution is relatively small. This is despite the fact that Richard Lynn has found that Northeast Asians have significantly higher average intelligence than Europeans, outscoring them by around 5 IQ points.[80]

Our proposed answer to the relative lack of genius among Northeast Asians is that they lack the Endogenous personality; presumably from having had a different historical environment than

---

[79] Murray, C. (2006). *Human Accomplishment: The Pursuit of Excellence in the Arts and Sciences, 800 BC to 1950.* New York: HarperCollins.

[80] Lynn, R. (2006). *Race Differences in Intelligence: An Evolutionary Analysis.* Augusta, GA: Washington Summit Publishers.

Europeans – an environment which imposed less intense and less sustained group *versus* group competition, and therefore less powerful *group* selection for creative innovation (i.e. natural selection for one group to gain an advantage over rival groups). Another possibility is that the environment of Northeast Asia was harsher, leading to stronger selection against Psychoticism and less genetic diversity as survivors would need to be very strongly adapted to the environment, leading to intelligence being bunched towards the mean. Accordingly, the chance occurrence of outlier intelligence combined with moderately high Psychoticism would be less than in Europe.[81] But this is a topic for future research.

---

[81] See, Dutton, E., te Nijenhuis, J. & Roivainen, E. (2014). Solving the puzzle of why Finns have the highest IQ but one of the lowest number of Nobel prizes in Europe. *Intelligence*, 46: 192-202 or Kura, K., te Nijenhuis, J. & Dutton, E. (2015). Why do Northeast Asians win so few Nobel Prizes? *Comprehensive Psychology,* 4.

Chapter Twelve

The Rise and Fall of Genius

The rise of genius

So far, we have discussed possible general mechanisms for the evolution of genius; and we have argued that genius is the characteristic outcome of the Endogenous personality who is highly self-motivated. But one of the most obvious and striking things about genius, is that there used to be a lot of geniuses – and major geniuses – and now there are very few.

The research in *Human Accomplishment* by Charles Murray, which is broadly confirmed by others,[82] indicates that genius in recent centuries has been essentially a phenomenon of the European population, including the diaspora of Europeans to other parts of the world. It seems that in Europe, and only in and around Europe and among its diaspora population, were the conditions necessary for the evolution of the Endogenous personality, who combines both very high general intelligence (g) and the 'inner'-orientated personality type.

---

[82] Woodley, M. A. (2012). The social and scientific temporal correlates of genotypic intelligence and the Flynn Effect. *Intelligence*, 40: 189-204.

The current evidence suggests that unusually high intelligence *but not the Endogenous personality* has also evolved in East Asia – indeed the intelligence is probably even higher than in Europe. There are plausible historical scenarios which explain how high intelligence can evolve by multi-generational, individual-level natural selection which favours the reproductive success of the most intelligent members of the population (assisted by sexual selection *via* assortative mating whereby the most intelligent men and women tend to marry each other, and women in polygamous societies sexually select for the higher status – and so usually more intelligent – men). Gregory Clark has described this (in great detail) for Europe, and Ron Unz (in outline) for China.[83]

But those aspects of adaptive high Psychoticism which are essential to the Endogenous personality seem only to have evolved in Europe, presumably due to the specific group selection factors. These could include between-group competition in a harsh environment; but one that is not *too* harsh, such that psychoticism and the chance occurrence of genius is all but eliminated. In addition, it is likely that the

---

[83] Clark, G. (2007) *Op. cit.*; Unz, R. (11 March 2013). How Social Darwinism Made Modern China. *The American Conservative.*
http://www.theamericanconservative.com/articles/how-social-darwinism-made-modern-china-248 Accessed 12 Aug 2015

Black Death of the fourteenth century, which killed up to half of Europeans but around 80% of the serfs,[84] provided a significant boost to European intelligence; since the most intelligent classes and groups suffered the lowest mortality rates.

At any rate, in England and later elsewhere in Europe, and from the Middle Ages onwards, there was a tremendous concentration of major, world-historical geniuses, and of major breakthroughs; which came thick and fast; and interacted in a synergistic fashion to trigger first an Agricultural (or Agrarian), then an Industrial Revolution accelerating from about 1700 and taking off about 1800. The result was a tremendous increase in agricultural efficiency and production, and the advent of a new form of social organization based on steam, iron and steel, machines, and transportation – which taken altogether reduced mortality rates, especially child mortality, and enabled rapid and massive population growth.

Our assumption – defended earlier in this book – is that breakthroughs require geniuses, even when the identity of these geniuses is not known or uncertain; as is often the case in agriculture.

Behind many of the breakthroughs of the modern world lies the principle of 'division of labour' which was first articulated by the Scottish philosopher Adam Smith (1723-1790). He

---

[84] Byrne, P. (2004). *The Black Death.* Westport: Greenwood.

recognized, described and promoted something that had already begun to happen. Division of labour entailed two things: that the work force should be subdivided to specialize in their functions, and that these specialized functions could be coordinated towards the final result. The result was – potentially – a *massive* increase in efficiency (output per unit of input) purely resulting from a change of social organization. Smith's example was a pin factory, where he showed that dividing the task of pin making into specialized functions and then coordinating these workers into a workshop or factory would lead to more than a two-hundred-fold greater number of pins: from a few *dozen* pins per man per day, to several *thousand* pins.

This is the essence of that increased productivity which defines the Industrial Revolution – more output for the same amount of input. Indeed, in agriculture the productivity increase went even further, with more production of food for less input of man-hours – meaning that, as well as supporting an increasing population size, much of the previously farming workforce was available to be redeployed into the new industries (indeed, they were more or less forced into the new industries in order to survive).

In agriculture there was enclosure of the large, open fields; effective crop rotations with new winter fodder plants (such as turnips) to sustain larger flocks and herds of animals; the use of manuring and liming to improve crop yields; the invention of selective animal breeding (i.e. accelerated natural selection supervised by men) which yielded more meat, wool, strength etc. from the same number of animals; and the invention of many new tools and machines (often using metal instead of wood) enabling fewer men to do more and a better standard of work.

We assume that each of these breakthroughs was enabled by one or more geniuses; and the combination of these multiple geniuses and breakthroughs was an increase in agricultural efficiency far beyond anything in the history of the world. Some of the contributing geniuses probably included people such as Coke of Norfolk, 'Turnip' Townsend (Charles, 2nd Viscount Townshend, 1674-1738), Jethro Tull (1674-1741), Robert Bakewell (1725-95) and many more.[85]

Increased food production partly enabled the Industrial Revolution, and was also enabled by it – so there were breakthroughs in coal mining (including division of labour and massive coordinated works), transportation (canals, railways,

---

[85] For an examination of the Industrial Revolution see, Deane, P. (1979). *The First Industrial Revolution.* Cambridge: Cambridge University Press. For the Agricultural Revolution, see: Overton, M. (1996). *Agricultural Revolution in England: The Transformation of the Agrarian Economy, 1500-1850.* Cambridge: Cambridge University Press.

roads), steam power, iron and steel production – also international trade and great improvements in ship-building, communication systems, and the *Pax Britannica* of military strength (especially naval strength) to enable international trade – which itself had the effect of increasing productivity by specialization and coordination, as was first understood by the English philosopher David Ricardo (1772-1823) in his 'law of comparative advantage'.

The geniuses who contributed to the Industrial Revolution are extremely numerous and better known than the Agrarians; a mere selection would include the likes of Trevithic and Watt with the steam engine, Bessamer (steel), Crompton ('Mule'), Hargreaves (Spinning Jenny), engineers such as George Stephenson, Telford, Macadam…

Indeed from the late Middle Ages and through the Renaissance – especially from about 1600 and accelerating – genius was more and more apparent in European sciences, art, music, literature, mathematics, philosophy… almost everywhere. And this continued through into the twentieth century, especially in the sciences – with an especially astonishing constellation of geniuses in physics topped by Einstein.

The decline of genius

There are a number of reasons to think that intelligence is in decline, and this has become more-and-more evident from the middle of the twentieth century until it is now difficult to deny – since there are very few acknowledged geniuses at all, and some fields without any. This is despite a much larger population, and much better facilities and opportunities.

It is not just the number of geniuses that have declined but their quality – so, for example, in the late 1800s-early 1900s there was Clark Maxwell, Einstein, Rutherford, Heisenberg, Schroedinger, Planck, Bohr, Dirac… and so on and so forth – but a hundred years later there are only a few elderly geniuses left. In biology/ biochemistry, which had its golden era as recently as the middle twentieth century, there are now only a handful of elderly greats left-over from those days – such as American James Watson, the co-discoverer of DNA, and Sidney Brenner, the South African experimental geneticist.

The same picture can be seen even more starkly in classical music – the nineteenth century had Beethoven, Schubert, Schumann, Mendelssohn, Chopin, Debussy, Berlioz, Weber, Verdi, Wagner, Mahler, Brahms… the list just goes on and on. In the early twentieth century there were a few leftovers in Schoenberg, Stravinsky and Richard Strauss and then... nothing.

In English poetry from the fifteenth century right up into the middle twentieth century there were probably always several, sometimes many, genius poets – but since the deaths of Phillip Larkin, John Betjeman and Robert Graves in 1984-5 there are none.

Such impressions are confirmed by systematic studies of exceptional individuals and major innovations, and throughout Europe and the European diaspora – there is a picture of decline – initially decline in *per capita* rates of genius production, followed by decline in absolute rates; and accompanied by a decline in the magnitude of geniuses.[86]

Why should this be? If the Endogenous personality is the genius type, and is composed mainly of intelligence and personality, the main explanation is likely to be declining average intelligence, with a downshift in the distribution of geniuses, and (because of the properties of near-normal distribution curves) a very substantial

---

[86] E.g. Huebner, J. (2005). A possible declining trend for worldwide innovation. *Technological Forecasting and Social Change* 72: 980–986. Woodley, M.A. (2012). The social and scientific temporal correlates of genotypic intelligence and the Flynn effect. *Intelligence* 40: 189-204.

decline in the number of people with very high intelligence.

And indeed that is exactly what we find: a large and rapid decline in general intelligence, insofar as intelligence can be measured objectively (not relatively).

Decline of intelligence due to the most intelligent having the fewest children

Since general intelligence has a high heritability (approximately 80 per cent), the well-known fact that the most intelligent people (especially the most intelligent women) have the fewest children – in other words the inverse correlation between intelligence and fertility – must tend to reduce average intelligence over the generations.

So, IQ test scores, and proxy measures of intelligence such as educational level, years of education, social class, income; are strongly negatively associated with fertility among women, and to a lesser extent among men. In other words, overall, the more intelligent the woman, the fewer children she will bear.[87]

This is particularly significant in the modern world where the childhood mortality rate has

---

[87] See, Lynn, R. (2011). *Dysgenics: Genetic Deterioration in Modern Populations.* London: Ulster Institute for Social Research.

declined from more than half of children dying before adulthood (even higher among the least intelligent) to about one per cent in Western countries. In other words, nearly all children who are born will now survive to adulthood, and premature mortality rates have become so low as to be almost irrelevant at the population level. Therefore, in recent generations, differences in reproductive success are almost entirely a matter of differences in fertility – the more babies that are born, the greater the reproductive success.

On top of this, since the middle 1960s the fertility among European populations has gone below replacement levels (modern replacement fertility is just above two children per woman – above two to account for premature mortality) – so the age-corrected population of Europeans has been declining for several decades. (This decline in numbers was temporarily masked by an increase in life expectancy – leading to an 'ageing population' with a median average age of Europeans being typically around the mid-forties and climbing).

Sub-fertility especially applies to intelligent women; for example, in recent decades more than a third of women college graduates have zero children – and most college graduates are women. The most intelligent and most highly-educated women have extremely few children on average – in Lewis Terman's follow-up studies of highly intelligent

Californians from the early twentieth century, the most intelligent women had only approximately half a child per woman: only about a quarter of the replacement rate.[88]

The extension of years of formal education and training into the middle and late twenties, resulting in greater and greater delays in initiating families (the average age of a woman having her *first* child in Britain is now about 30); combined with increased involvement of women in the workforce (a trend that has been strongly encouraged both by radical feminism and by capitalism), seems to have had a particularly lethal effect on reproduction of intelligent women.

This change to extreme sub-fertility among the most intelligent seems to be due to several specific factors working together. One is surely secularism and the decline of religion, which is most evident among the most intelligent.[89] Even under modern conditions, traditional patriarchal religions often have above replacement fertility[90] – sometimes very high rates of fertility – so *religion can be an*

---

[88] Terman, L. (1959). *The Gifted Group at Mid-Life: Thirty Five Years Follow-up of the Superior Child*. Stanford: Stanford University Press.

[89] See, Dutton (2014). Op. cit.

[90] Rowthorn, R. (2011). Religion, fertility and genes: A dual inheritance model. *Proceedings of the Royal Society (B) Biological Sciences*. DOI: 10.1098/rspb.2010.2504

antidote to subfertility, but it is one which that is seldom used by the most intelligent.

Also important is the rise of contraception, the easy availability of multiple methods of contraception, and its social acceptability – in a context where contraception is more efficiently used by the more intelligent, who would be less impulsive anyway. The legalization and mass usage of abortion is a factor in enabling the decline of birth rates into sub-fertility, although probably not a factor in differential fertility by intelligence.

There are other more general factors, such as a more stable environment – meaning there is no need to have lots of children, so large families will tend to accidental, and underpinned by impulsiveness and thus low intelligence. These adverse trends were probably compounded by a dysgenic accumulation of deleterious mutations caused by the relaxation of mutation filtering from natural selection, mostly caused by the sharp decline in child mortality rates.

In sum, there seems little doubt that the pattern of differential reproduction in relation to intelligence must have had an effect on reducing average intelligence.

Measuring the decline of intelligence

It is one thing knowing that in principle intelligence must be declining; but the problem is that IQ testing is not suitable for measuring long term trends. An IQ questionnaire is a relative measure: it puts people into rank order by their test results – but it does not give an objective measure of intelligence levels.

In other words, IQ testing is like running races and placing people into first, second, third positions etc., but never using a stopwatch. This makes it impossible to know, over the decades, whether people are running faster, slower or staying the same. What is needed is some kind of objective measure of intelligence: a stopwatch.

This limitation in IQ testing led to the idea by one of this book's authors (Bruce G. Charlton) of measuring long term trends in intelligence using exactly a stopwatch measure: in other words studying the historical changes in the simple reaction time (sRT) measurement; because reaction times have been measured since the late 1800s, and provide an objective correlate of general intelligence.

Simple reaction times (sRT) typically involve something like pressing a button as rapidly as possible in response to a light coming-on, and measuring the time taken – this procedure usually takes some small fraction of a second: i.e. some few hundreds of milliseconds. Such reaction times are well known to be correlated with 'g' (general intelligence). While the correlation with intelligence is not large, sRTs have the great advantage of being objective and quantitative physiological measures – they are more like measuring height or blood pressure than getting people to do an IQ test (which is essentially a form of exam).

Working with Charlton, Michael Woodley discovered an already-published survey of historical reaction time data that demonstrated a striking slowing of sRTs from the time of Francis Galton in the late nineteenth century until the late 20th century. This data carried the strong implication that there had been a rapid and substantial decline in intelligence over the past hundred-plus years – and opened-up a new field of research which Woodley has been actively pursuing ever since.

This initial finding, which Charlton published on his blog, has since been improved, replicated and confirmed by Woodley and his colleagues[91] who

[91] Charlton, B.G & Woodley, M.A. Objective and direct evidence of 'dysgenic' decline in genetic 'g' (IQ). Bruce Charlton's Miscellany blog - charltonteaching.blogspot.co.uk posted on 28 February 2012, also Charlton, B.G. Taking on-board that the Victorians were more intelligent than us. Posted on 23 June 2012; Woodley, M. A., te Nijenhuis, J. & Murphy, R. (2013). Were the Victorians cleverer than us?: The decline in general intelligence estimated from a meta-analysis of the

have deployed other convergent methods for indirectly measuring long term intelligence changes.[92] Using reaction time data, the decline in genotypic IQ is of-the-order of 1.5 IQ points per decade – that is about 15 points, or one standard deviation, in a century; and probably more, over the past two hundred years. [93] To put this in perspective,

---

slowing of simple reaction time. *Intelligence,* 41: 843-850. See also: Woodley, M. A.; Madison, G. & Charlton, B. (2014). Possible dysgenic trends in simple visual reaction time performance in the Scottish Twenty-07 cohort: a reanalysis of Deary and Der (2005). *The Mankind Quarterly*, 55: 110-124; Woodley, M. A. & Figueredo, A. J. (2013). *Historical Variability in Heritable General Intelligence.* Buckingham: University of Buckingham Press.

[92] For example, they have found a secular decline in the use of difficult words, difficult word use being a proxy for intelligence. Woodley of Menie, M.A.; Fernandes, H.; Figueredo, A.J. & Meisenberg, G. (2015). By their words ye shall know them: Evidence of genetic selection against general intelligence and concurrent environmental enrichment in vocabulary usage since the mid-19th century. *Frontiers in Psychology*, 6: 361. They have also noted a decline in colour discrimination, which itself g-loaded. See, Woodley of Menie, M.A., & Fernandes, H.B.F. (2015). Showing their true colors: Secular declines and a Jensen effect on color acuity – more evidence for the weaker variant of Spearman's other hypothesis. *Personality & Individual Differences*. In press.

[93] Charlton, B.G. What is the main selection mechanism causing the 'dysgenic' decline in intelligence over the past couple of centuries? Intelligence, Personality and Genius blog - iqpersonalitygenius.blogspot.co.uk. Posted on 7 February 2013; Woodley, M. A. (2014). How fragile is our intellect? Estimat-

15 points would be approximately the difference in average IQ between a low level security guard (85) and a police constable (100), or between a high school science teacher (115) and a biology professor at an elite university (130).

In other words, in terms of intelligence, the average Englishman from about 1880-1900 would be in roughly the top 15 per cent of the population in 2000 – and the difference would be even larger if we extrapolated back further towards about 1800 when the Industrial Revolution began to initiate massive demographic changes in the British population (although this was a time before reaction time measures existed).

These numbers are not intended to be precise – indeed real precision (in the sense of exact accuracy in averages and measures of scatter around averages) is not available in IQ studies for many reasons to do with the difficulties of truly random and sufficiently large population sampling, lack of a full range of unbiased and objective data; and the fact the IQ points are not on a 'ratio scale' but are derived from putting a population sample into rank order on the basis of (usually) one-off testing.

---

ing losses in general intelligence due to both selection and mutation accumulation. *Personality and Individual Differences*, 75: 80-84. These are early and approximate attempts at quantifying intelligence losses due to mutation accumulation.

However, the take-home message is that there has been a large and important decline in the average intelligence of Western populations over the past century and more. In every day terms; the academics of the year 2000 were the school teachers of 1900, the school teachers of the year 2000 would have been the factory workers (the average people) of 1900, the office workers and policemen of 2000 were the farm labourers of 1900, while the low level security guards and shop assistants of 2000 were probably in the workhouse, on the streets or dead in 1900.

The substantial long-term unemployed or unemployable, chronically sick or physically/ psychologically disabled, dependent 'underclass' of 2000, simply didn't exist in 1900. And even this estimate is ignoring the expansion of education since 1900, which expanded the middle class occupations and would, in itself, reduce the average intelligence of academics and teachers in 2000 compared to 1900.

But what about the Flynn effect?

Objective measures show that intelligence has declined rapidly and substantially over the past century or two; but it is also true that the so-called 'Flynn Effect' has been evident.

This name refers to the fact that IQ raw scores (i.e. the results on IQ tests, the proportion of correct answers) have been rising throughout the 20th century in Western countries.[94] So, performance in IQ tests has been increasing at the same time as real, underlying general intelligence has been decreasing.

This can happen because IQ score is a relative, not an absolute, measure of intelligence – and because it is essentially the result of a timed examination involving answering questions. There are likely to be many reasons for increasing IQ scores, indeed any reason for increased exam scores might be contributory – for example improved health, cultural change, educational expansion, socialization of testing procedures, test question and format familiarity, teaching of test strategies, increased use of multiple choice formats (where guessing is encouraged), probably also increased levels of cheating – all may contribute variously to IQ test scores rising even as intelligence declined.

But even the Flynn effect has now plateaued or gone into reverse in a number of countries,[95] and the rise in scores have been shown to be occurring most on the least g-loaded parts of the tests.[96] So, general

---

[94] Flynn, J. R. (2012). *Are We Getting Smarter? Rising IQ in the Twenty First Century*. Cambridge: Cambridge University Press.

[95] See, Dutton, E. & Lynn, R. (2015). A negative Flynn Effect in France, 1999-2008/9. *Intelligence,* 51: 67-70.

[96] Flynn, Op. cit.

intelligence has been declining substantially and rapidly *even though* IQ test scores used to be increasing.

Furthermore, it seems likely that while underlying intelligence was much higher in the past, the measurable intellectual performance – for example in examinations, intelligence tests, and in real life situations – of most people was severely damaged by lack of education, harsh physical conditions such as cold and damp, starvation, disease, exhaustion and endemic severe infectious disease, pain and disabilities and so on. Such factors would be expected substantially to reduce (or abolish) many aspects of intellectual performance in difficult tasks by (for example) impairing concentration and motivation.

Imagine doing an IQ test, an examination, or attempting any challenging intellectual activity such as reading a difficult book or performing calculations; while suffering with a fever or chronic pain or gnawed by hunger: imagine suffering fevers, pain, or hunger continuously for most of your life... but this was the normal situation for most of the population in earlier times. No matter what their underlying level of intelligence might be, their performance was significantly impaired for much of the time.

High-IQ genes versus low-IQ genes

At a genetic level, intelligence may in principle reduce because of a reduction in high intelligence genes in a population and/or as an accumulation of intelligence-damaging mutations in the population.

Differential fertility would lead to a decline in intelligence by a reduction in the proportion of high IQ genes in the population. This happens from a combination of the relatively less intelligent people having on average the most children, and the most intelligent people having very low fertility. Since the most intelligent people are sub-fertile, with less than two offspring per woman, the genes which have made them the most intelligent will decline in each generation – first declining as a proportion of the gene pool, and then declining in absolute prevalence.

For instance, when there is a woman with ultra-high intelligence who has zero children (which is the most usual outcome among ultra-intelligent women), then whatever it was about her genes which made her so intelligent is eliminated from the gene pool: this is the loss of 'high-IQ genes'.[97]

---

[97] In terms of 'IQ genes', it has been found that the possession of a particular allele on Chromosome 6 increases IQ by around 4 points. See, Chorley, M. J., M. Seese, M. J. Owen, et al. (1998). A quantitative trait locus associated with cognitive ability in children. *Psychological Science*, 9: 159-166.

But our suggestion of mutation accumulation is that there is an additional mechanism of an accumulation of what could be termed 'low-IQ genes'. To be clear: these are not genes coding for low intelligence – rather they are damaged genes which pathologically reduce intelligence. So, as well as there being a decline in intelligence from the reduced proportion of 'high-IQ' genes, there is also an increase in the proportion of 'low IQ genes' in the population.

High IQ genes have (presumably) been selected for in the past because they increased intelligence, and thereby (under ancestral – especially Medieval – conditions) increased reproductive success.

But low IQ genes are not, in general, a product of natural selection: rather they are spontaneously occurring deleterious mutations, which happen with every generation due to any cause of genetic damage (e.g. electromagnetic radiation, chemical damage), or errors in replication.

These mutations will, if not eliminated, accumulate generation upon generation. Therefore when they have accumulated, the low-IQ genes were not 'selected for'; rather it was a matter of *lack of* selection, relaxation of natural selection. 'Low IQ gene' therefore usually means something like a genetic mutation that – in potentially a wide range of ways, by impairing almost any aspect of brain structure, organization or functioning –

actively damages brain processing speed and efficiency, hence reducing general intelligence.

In technical terms, the selection mechanism for eliminating these spontaneously accumulating low IQ genes is mutation-selection balance. The idea is that mutations spontaneously occur and need selectively to be eliminated. In other words, by some means, those organisms which have damaging mutations must (on average) fail to reproduce – must indeed *be prevented from reproducing* – so they will not hand-on the mutations to the next generation, and contaminate the gene pool with mutations.

Conversely, only a small proportion of the population – i.e. those with good genes – are allowed (by the selective environment) to reproduce; and typically this minority will provide nearly all of the next generation.

Since there are new mutations each generation, as well as the possibility of some inherited from parents, the process needs to be perfect over the long term, otherwise the accumulation of damaging mutations will eventually prevent reproduction and damage survival to cause extinction. The term for such extinction is *mutational meltdown* – and this has been observed to occur in some lower organisms, especially when mutations are accumulating and the population is reducing. This probably happens in some inbred captive populations such as in zoos, as well as in modern human society.

The term mutation-selection balance refers to the fact that the occurrence of mutations must be balanced by the elimination of mutations: natural selection (including sexual selection – mate choice) must be powerful enough to sieve-out all the deleterious mutations. If natural selection is not strong enough to do this, then mutations will accumulate, brain function will be damaged, and intelligence will decline.

Each spontaneous mutation has about a fifty-fifty chance of damaging brain function, because the brain depends on a very high proportion of genes to develop normally and make its structural components, its proteins, enzymes, hormones, neurotransmitters and so on. Thus the brain is a large 'mutational target' (as Geoffrey Miller has termed it) – and will usually show up, in a quantitative fashion, the amount of mutational damage a person has. In other words, high intelligence requires 'Good Genes' – where good genes means a genome low in mutations; conversely a high mutational load will cause low intelligence.

Before the Industrial Revolution, individuals with a higher mutational load, which means a higher load of low-IQ genes (and therefore lower intelligence) had lower-than-average reproductive success due to very high (indeed, probably near total) childhood mortality rates. But since the child mortality rates fell from more than half to about one per cent in most of Europe, almost all babies that are born have survived to adulthood, and most of them have reproduced. Therefore, we must assume that there have by now been several generations – in England at least eight generations – of mutation accumulation. And we must also assume that this has had a significant effect in reducing intelligence.

This produces what is truly a 'dysgenic' effect on intelligence, since it is not evolved, not adaptive, not a new ability – but instead a lowering of intelligence due to a pathological process; a destruction of adaptive human intelligence caused by an accumulation of damage.

And although intelligence decline is a sensitive measure of mutation accumulation – it is not the only consequence. Many other human adaptations would be destroyed by mutation accumulation – including evolved human personality types. As well as pulling down human intelligence; mutation accumulation would be expected to destroy the Endogenous personality, to impair human creativity – and would be a further nail in the coffin of genius.

Decline of intelligence due to mutation accumulation

So, the decline of intelligence that has now been measured using reaction times and confirmed with other methods, has been too fast, and gone too far, fully to be accounted for by the mechanism of differences in fertility between most and least intelligent.

To re-emphasize; we have no doubt that this mechanism of differential fertility has had an effect in reducing intelligence over the past two hundred years, but there must be other additional explanations for so great and rapid a decline in intelligence – a decline (we argue) that has been sufficient to all-but eliminate world class geniuses from the European population, and hence the world.

We therefore suggest that the main additional mechanism to reduce intelligence may plausibly be the generation-by-generation accumulation of deleterious genetic mutations; as a result of the near-elimination of historically high child mortality rates which used-to clear mutations from the gene pool with each generation.[98]

But after the Industrial Revolution got going, mortality rates declined for the least intelligent

---

[98] Hamilton, W. D. (2002). The hospitals are coming. Chapter in *Narrow Roads of Gene Land* – Volume 2. Oxford, UK: Oxford University Press.

along with everyone else; so that even the poorest families usually raised several-to-many children, then there was a *double-whammy* dysgenic effect: a reduced proportion of high IQ genes with each generation (due to progressively lowering fertility among the higher IQ) and also an increasing accumulation of low IQ genes (intelligence-damaging deleterious mutations) with each generation.

In sum, since the Industrial Revolution, individuals with the greatest mutational load (IQ-harmful genes) have been initially been above-replacement fertile (having on average more than 2 surviving children per woman, for the first time in history perhaps), and also differentially more fertile than those with the least mutational load. And compared with 150-200 years ago, there is now a lower proportion (and a lowering absolute amount) of IQ-enhancing genes in the gene pool of England, plus a higher proportion and accumulation of deleterious IQ-damaging mutations. And this double-whammy effect is, we think, why average general intelligence has declined so rapidly and so much in England over the past couple of centuries.

Historical trends in the prevalence of genius

So, the first effect of the 'perfect storm' of English geniuses (also probably seen, although not yet documented, in several other European nations such as France and Germany) was to expand the population and thereby increase the number of English geniuses; but as the generations went by, the adverse selection factors and mutation accumulation would have 'sabotaged' the expansion of geniuses by reducing the average intelligence in the population – firstly the proportion, and then the actual number, of people of very high intelligence, so that the number of new geniuses occurring dwindled into again being extremely rare and 'one off'.

As a consequence, it has been documented by Woodley and others that the number of 'breakthrough' macro-inventions – major inventions that really alter how we live – has decreased markedly since the Victorian Era, though there are still many micro-inventions, which are merely tinkering with macro-inventions.[99]

For example, a macro-innovation like the computer was invented by geniuses (such as Babbage, Turing and von Neumann) up to the middle twentieth century; and the multiple improvements in miniaturization, processing speed and memory etc. – which have made the computer so widely useful – are classified as micro-

---

[99] Woodley, M. A. (2012). The social and scientific temporal correlates of genotypic intelligence and the Flynn Effect. *Intelligence,* 40: 189-204.

innovations, and were made by a multitude of people and organizations, often employing 'trial and error' type methods.

So, micro-innovations are extremely important, and make a big difference, and take some decades to emerge –the fact is that micro-innovations are not so difficult as macro-innovations. In particular micro-innovations do not require such exceptionally creative people as macro-innovations – but instead can emerge from knowledge accumulation, high-normal levels of cleverness, communication, and routine 'research and development'.

The importance of genius in human history – and specifically in modern society – is that we argue that it was the uniquely high number and concentration of geniuses in the European population that triggered and sustained the Industrial Revolution. Genius-generated macro-innovations provided the foundation for amplification by numerous micro-innovations; and the combination supported an expansion in world population from about one to seven billion, and still growing.

As intelligence declines, the foundations for this socio-economic system will be removed. The breakthrough-upon-breakthrough needed to provide and sustain growth will presumably be the first to dry up. Then there will be a period of plateau when people can continue to exploit and marginally-improve upon the successes of the past – some decades as micro-innovations are developed. (These stages are probably already behind us.)

But as intelligence continues to decline, then growth in productivity will reverse into decline and inefficiency, as the ability of people to sustain, repair, even to maintain, the highly technical, specialized and coordinated world civilization will be lost, just as occurred with the fall of Western Roman civilization; when agricultural and industrial production and trade all collapsed, the standard of living and population plummeted, and general technical and organizational levels took more than a millennium to recover.

When the supply of major geniuses becomes inadequate, or dries-up altogether, then the past two to three centuries of world productivity growth – which depended on a continual stream of major discoveries – one innovation making possible another, one repairing the problems generated by another, and all of them interacting to enable further innovation… all this will come to an end. And since modernity (the socio-economic system since the Industrial Revolution) depends on growth – specifically growth in capability and efficiency/ productivity – then modernity will first halt, then reverse.

Arguably this reversal has already happened in The West, and we are now living off capital – well embarked on a downslope of reduced societal efficiency which affects all nations (because the innovations and breakthroughs created by geniuses of European origin have usually spread to the rest of the world).

So, we believe that the end of the 'age of genius' entails the end of modernity – the end of the type of society that has dominated and spread across the world since the Agricultural and Industrial Revolutions; whether the cause is that we have run out of geniuses, or because (as some people argue) we have merely run out of major things for geniuses to discover. Either way, the consequences are the same: the collapse of modernity, which absolutely depends on a steady supply of geniuses and breakthroughs – and reversion to pre-Industrial Revolution conditions, of one sort or another.

Chapter Thirteen

The neglect and suppression of genius

Genius and the educational system

The Genius Triad is intelligence, intuitive creativity and long-term self-motivation – all focused on the same domain. Psychologically the triad could be termed Questing Creative Intelligence; and QCI will be found not only among potential geniuses of the major type, but also with lower strength among small-scale geniuses, more local or partial geniuses; who, although capable of far less than the likes of Rutherford, George Stephenson or Alan Turing; nonetheless will work for, and tend to make, original breakthroughs. It is up to other people whether these breakthroughs are noticed, understood and used; or (as so often happens at present) ignored, vilified and suppressed.

With the decline in average intelligence, and the resulting decline of genius, society becomes ever more short-term oriented and politically less stable as these factors have been shown to be underpinned by national intelligence. Richard Lynn and Finnish political scientist Tatu Vanhanen (1929-2015), for example, have shown that numerous measures of civilization – education level, sanitation, democracy (and so smooth transfers of power), political stability, and lack of crime and corruption – are all moderately to strongly predicted by national IQ.[100] And they have shown that these national IQs are highly reliable as they strongly correlate with national measures of proxies for IQ, such as international student assessments.

In a society of declining intelligence, we would expect: rising crime and corruption; decreasing civic participation and lower voter turn-out; higher rates of illegitimacy; poorer health and greater obesity, an increased interest in the instinctive, especially sex; greater political instability and decline in democracy; higher levels of social conflict; higher levels of selfishness and so a decline in any welfare state; a growing unemployable underclass; falling educational standards; and a lack of intellectualism and thus decreasing interest in education as a good in itself. We would also expect more and more little things to go wrong that we didn't used to notice: buses running out of petrol, trains delayed, aeroplanes landing badly, roads not being repaired, people arriving late and thinking it's perfectly okay; several large and lots of little lies . . .

---

[100] Lynn R. & Vanhanen, T. (2012). *Intelligence: A Unifying Construct for the Social Sciences.* London: Ulster Institute for Social Research.

In addition, the broader modern system – especially of extended formal education (stretching ever further into adult life), exam results and continuous assessments, required subjects and courses; the supposed 'meritocracy' – suppresses the influence of genius, since the Endogenous personality is seeking, ever more strongly with age, to follow his inner drives, his Destiny, and all the paraphernalia of normal, standard requirements stands in his path. While others need sticks and carrots, and are grateful for encouragement, discipline and direction; the Endogenous personality is driven from within and (beyond a basic minimum) he neither needs nor appreciates these things – at best they slow him down, at worst they thwart and exclude him. The Endogenous personality requires mainly to be *allowed* to do what he intrinsically and spontaneously wants to do – but in modern society he is more likely to be prevented.

Creative people always have difficult personalities; and conversely nice people with conscientious, obedient reliable personalities are not creative. This means that institutions, employers and patrons *must* tolerate the difficulties of Endogenous personalities, if they want those things done that only geniuses can do. Most of the time, potential geniuses are a nuisance – but there are times when such people are essential.

However, in order to do these things geniuses, have to find themselves a job or a university place or a patron. In a less meritocratic society, this might be *via* family connections or informally demonstrating one's genius. In other words, the difficult short term decision to appoint, tolerate, perhaps even reward an asocial Endogenous personality instead of a conscientious and popular Head Girl type might be made by an individual who knew the nature and potential of the Endogenous personality (perhaps because he was himself an Endogenous personality).

But, nowadays, such decisions are usually made by committee vote, by officials and bureaucrats who are themselves usually the opposite of geniuses; and done according to guidelines and protocols – 'standard procedures' and an attitude of risk-minimization will almost invariably tend to exclude geniuses, who are nearly always lop-sided with weaknesses as well as strengths, and each a one-off in terms of aptitude.

The Endogenous personality combines high intelligence with the 'inner' personality; and it used to be fairly normal for Endogenous personalities to gain admittance to the most elite institutions. However, nowadays, it is clear that college admission criteria are much less likely to select for intelligence than in the past. In other words, attendance at the most selective institutions is no longer a matter of being of the highest intelligence. Partly this is because of the changing nature of educational evaluations – the best reports and grades at school or top performance in exams are no longer so 'g-loaded' that is, they are less correlated with general intelligence than they used to be (some of this may be due to the IQ test score inflation which is termed 'the Flynn Effect').

But it seems certain that 'elite' modern institutions are not evaluating and selecting primarily on the basis of intelligence – since they do not use intelligence tests, high intelligence is only selected-for insofar as it correlates with the educational, personal and other assessments which are used for selection – and the correlation between these and intelligence is not close (around 0.5 for high school achievement), and much less close than it used to be.

Nor are the elite modern institutions selecting for personality qualities of independent and inner motivations and evaluations that are an intrinsic part of the Endogenous personality – quite the opposite, in fact; since there are multiple preferences and quotas in place which net exclude European-descended men (that group with *by far* the highest proportion of Endogenous personalities – i.e. having the ultra-high intelligence and creative personality type). This can be seen in explicit group preference policies and campaigns enforced by government (and the mass media), and informal (covert) preferences – leading to ratios and compositions at elite institution (especially obvious in STEM subjects: i.e. Science, Technology, Engineering, Medicine) that demonstrate grossly lower proportions of European-descended men than would result from selecting for the Endogenous personality type.

Indeed modern institutions are not even trying to select primarily by intelligence – the reality of which they often deny; but instead are implicitly – by the nature of their evaluations – and also by explicitly-stated policies – selecting on other grounds, especially for the 'Head Girl' personality – the conscientious, empathic, socially integrated all-rounders. Modern society is, of course, run by Head Girls, of both sexes (plus a smattering of charming or charismatic psychopaths), hence there is no assigned place for the creative genius. Modern colleges aim at recruiting Head Girls, so do universities, so does science, so do the arts, so does the mass media, so does the legal profession, so does medicine, so does the military. And in doing so, except insofar as they make errors; they filter-out and exclude even the *possibility* of creative genius.[101]

---

[101] See: Charlton, B. G. (2009). Why are modern scientists so dull? How science selects for perseverance and sociability at the expense of intelligence and creativity. *Medical Hypothe-*

If a creative genius does somehow happen to get-through, by error or accident – that is, someone who can recognize the Endogenous personality and may be expected to favour it – then he will not in practice be allowed to select more of his type; because of the way that all significant decisions are taken by committees (dominated by Head Girl types) and controlled by checklists, guidelines and protocols. These will have been designed, and are enforced, by Head Girl types with the aim of excluding those who do not conform to what is 'normally' required (thereby excluding those who are better than normal, along with those who are worse than normal).

As a result of the above trends, the most intelligent and the most creative people are nowadays dispersed among variously ranked institutions (and no-institutions-at-all); and typically have sub-optimal – sometimes frankly bad – academic and employment records. The Endogenous personalities are very seldom to be found in the most prestigious, best-funded, or fashionable subjects (unless they were the original founders of the field, or perhaps at a low level or in

---

ses. 72: 237-243; and Charlton, B. G. (2009). Sex ratios in the most-selective elite US undergraduate colleges and universities are consistent with the hypothesis that modern educational systems increasingly select for conscientious personality compared with intelligence. *Medical Hypotheses.* 73: 127-129.

a marginal capacity) – since a genius is stubbornly self-motivated, and will work only where his destiny leads him (and he may refuse or neglect work that interferes with his destiny). The fields in which genius is questing are as various as the people with genius; and will often strike other people as futile or absurd; nonetheless, 'eccentricity' is intrinsic to the necessary autonomy of genius.

Genius and societal self-interest

The reason for society to tolerate and sustain geniuses is not that geniuses deserve more concern than other kinds of people – the bottom-line reason is societal self-interest.

Geniuses are 'for' the good of the human group; they are people with a special gift for solving specially-difficult problems; and all human societies are confronted – sooner or later and usually sooner – by the kinds of problems that can only be solved by geniuses; lacking-which, the problems are simply not solved. British mathematician Alan Turing's (1912-1954) cracking of the Enigma code – portrayed in the 2014 film *The Imitation Game* is a case in point. This intensely difficult man had to struggle against Head Girl types to get a job for the government and then to build his code-cracking machine. But if there had been no Turing, the War would have lasted significantly longer, with terrible consequences.[102]

To reiterate, geniuses are people who combine an especially high intellectual ability with a spontaneous tendency to focus on some abstract (by 'abstract' we mean 'not-social') problem, and the inner motivation to maintain this focus, to quest for an answer, for relatively long periods of time. However, there are only two ways that they can realistically find the space to pursue their genius: a patron or, in some cases, a well-funded university.

Indeed, if the genius can become an academic he is confronted with further problems. Once upon a time, he could do occasional teaching and then

---

[102] For a biography of Turing, see: Hodges, A. (2012). *Alan Turing: The Enigma.* Princeton: Princeton University Press. Turing, like many other geniuses, was an Endogenous personality subtype that also fitted into the Asperger's syndrome type of personality which has in recent decades been rediscovered and elucidated especially in the work of Uta Frith and Simon Baron Cohen, for example Frith, U. (1991) *Autism and Asperger's Syndrome.* Cambridge, UK: Cambridge University Press; Baron-Cohen, S. (1995) *Mindblindness: an Essay on Autism and Theory of Mind*, Cambridge, MA, USA: MIT Press/Bradford Books. The relationship between Asperger's syndrome and the Endogenous personality requires further elucidation than we can give it here; but in a nutshell the two definitions overlap and individuals, including geniuses like Newton, Turing or Godel may share features of both. But one may be present without the other – for instance, the Endogenous personality may be sociable, while Asperger's is not necessarily creative.

devote himself to his research, publishing if he discovered anything. Now, there is constant pressure to publish, publish in certain journals, attend conferences (Hellish social events for geniuses), and obtain research grants. This would drive many geniuses out of academia, leaving it dominated by the Head Girls.

To read of such difficult, annoying, disruptive geniuses as mathematical physicist Paul Dirac (1902-1984; who almost never spoke)[103] or the philosopher Ludwig Wittgenstein (1889-1951; who refused to socialize or even eat with colleagues, or do administration; and taught only the people he wanted to teach and in exactly the way he wanted to teach them),[104] and then to realize that these were Professors at the world-leading University of Cambridge – is to recognize that such characters would nowadays get nowhere near a Cambridge chair or any other chair (not least because actual ability to perform at a really high level in one's subject or function, is no longer regarded as of primary importance in modern British universities, or indeed anywhere else in Britain).

Where instead do such men find themselves? The answer is not known for sure – but anecdotal

---

[103] See, Farmelo, G. (2009). *The Strangest Man: The Hidden Life of Paul Dirac, Quantum Genius*. London: Faber & Faber.
[104] See, Monk, R. (2012). *Ludwig Wittgenstein: The Duty of Genius*. New York: Random House.

information and our personal knowledge suggests that they are scattered in multiple and various marginal and low status circumstances, where their potentially vital work is assiduously ignored, mocked or attacked – and this endemic and chronic hostility sooner-or-later tends to have a knock-on, deleterious, distorting effect on their attitudes and output; inducing a bitterness, pride, aggressive irritability, a siege mentality, despair and inertia – or some other wholly-understandable but profoundly unhelpful and achievement-destructive frame of mind.

Meanwhile, compliant, careerist, sociable mediocrity is zealously enforced by the ruling Head Girl types; whose primary, often sole, concern is their own social micro-environment. And as average intelligence has declined, two things have happened that have had a major impact on the university.

Firstly, the ideal of the pursuit of truth has been replaced by the pursuit of an ideology. And secondly, the idea that education is a good in itself – an intellectual idea, requiring honesty, personal dedication, and long term thinking in terms of the future and nature of society – has disappeared; to be replaced by the view that it is a means to an end, a way of getting a certificate, making money, having a 'party' lifestyle – things in which the potential genius is not really interested (and should not become interested).

So colleges and universities – which used to be a haven for geniuses – have instead become a mixture of ideological churches; holiday camps; schools of dissipation and irresponsibility; 'learning shops' run by managers, accountants and public relations professionals; and research factories generating 'evidence' as required by whomsoever has money enough to fund them.

Thus in Britain, and in all the other European and European diaspora nations (the USA, Canada, Australia etc.); we see the same picture of a society with a high concentration of effective geniuses that flipped, quite suddenly – and in the space of a generation or two – into a society which is in practice, and almost universally, actively anti-genius: a society selecting against genius, excluding of genius, persecuting of genius.

Fake creativity

Although the picture is one of an extraordinarily rapid decline in the prevalence of geniuses, the trend has been confused and clouded by the simple expedient of re-labelling and denial.

By re-labelling, some non-creative nonentity (maybe someone of high career status, maybe of high but un-creative ability, maybe a charming character, maybe just a novelty-merchant) is simply *stated to be a genius*, repeatedly talked about as a genius – probably given awards and medals for being a genius – and the concept of genius is thereby blurred, relativized and even further discredited.

By denial we mean the common notion among sophisticated modern people that 'geniuses' are no different from anyone else – the denial that there is indeed such a thing as a genius – that the whole thing is a matter of luck or labelling, or a cult of personality, or romanticism – or part of an hierarchical (and probably patriarchal) conspiracy. By the end of this deconstruction and subversion, the disappearance of genius has been disguised by denying that there ever was genius, and the whole thing relativized into a matter of professional eminence, or even just fame or notoriety – so the latest 'shocking' novelist is actually, basically, the same as Shakespeare; the latest art gallery 'installation' doing the same thing as a Rembrandt portrait or a Rodin sculpture.

This can be seen most obviously in fields where, by the evaluative standards of a century ago, there are no living geniuses at all. For example classical music, fine art, and poetry (in English).

Worse still, 'originality' – rather than consequence – has become the test of genius. The fact that something is 'original' – meaning *novel*, makes it praise-worthy. In fact, originality has now become indistinguishable from mere changes of fashion.

In previous eras, there was not a special status given to novelty as an aspect of high quality work – but since about 1800 in the West there has been: greatness is supposedly mostly a matter of being innovative. Yet while great geniuses may innovate this is not the rule, for instance Gluck and J.C. Bach were greater innovators, but much lesser composers than, J.S. Bach and Mozart; Constable and Gainsborough were less original, but higher quality, painters than Francis Bacon or Lucien Freud.

Therefore we currently have an incentive system in place to generate *fake* creativity: an incentive system in which there are un-creative people who dishonestly strive to be regarded as original because they want to appropriate the label of creative and usurp the title of 'genius'. In sum, under modernity creativity has been reduced to novelty – and novelty can be simulated.

It is trivially easy for clever and well-trained people to generate mere novelty, so there is an excess of it (we call it 'fashion'). Therefore the discriminative test applied to novelties is whether they are approved by the social systems that allocate high status. When novelty is socially approved, then the person who generated it gets to be called creative – maybe even a creative genius.

The Genius Famine

Thus: Novelty of outcome + Social Approval of that outcome = Fake creativity

And fake creativity is an attribute *bestowed* upon an outcome or person; bestowed by the social systems for generating status – in other words the mass media (primarily), politics, civil administration, the legal system, education... in a nutshell the Leftist Establishment.

We regard it as quite obvious and undeniable that the Establishment is now 'Leftist' as evidenced by dominance of those with this perspective in academia, among senior churchmen, in the media, and in all mainstream political parties – all of which promote some degree of Political Correctness. The radicals of the 1960s, and their followers, are the honour-loaded Establishment of today. The British philosopher Sean Gabb has documented how, since the 1960s, the Left has displaced the traditional 'conservative' Establishment, taking over almost all of organs on the British State, including the police and legal system.[105] The dominance of Leftism in academia has been documented in numerous studies.[106]

---

[105] For analysis of the degree to which Political Correctness controls these aspects of modern Britain see Gabb, S. (2007). *Culture Revolution, Culture War: How the Conservatives Lost England and How to Get it Back.* London: Hampden Press.

[106] Rothman, S., L. Lichter, & N. Nevitte. (2005). Politics and Professional Advancement among College Faculty. *The Forum* 3: 1.

So, as would be expected, political correctness has captured creativity – and replaced real creativity with a fake creativity which is controlled by the arbiters of modernity: that is, mostly the mass media. So modern 'creatives' are celebrated for their subversion of (or exposure of the supposed hypocrisy of) traditional, bourgeois and religious values; and rewarded for their celebrations of equality, pacifism, rebellion, feminism, sexual experimentation, antiracism, multiculturalism, and the rest of it...

This matter of being able to define/ bestow the accolade of creativity is of extreme importance to the modern intellectual establishment – indeed, fake creativity stands close to the heart of the ideological project of the modern (Leftist) elite – because the Left works mainly via manipulations of esteem, including self-esteem. Its enemies are portrayed as immoral (especially 'selfish,' judgemental or 'racist' and thus associated with the Nazis and their horrors) and of low intelligence, knuckle-dragging crudity, retardation and/ or lunacy.

Thus to claim to be a 'creative' person has been changed from being the mere observation of a psychological fact; to an arrogant claim of deserving high social status for having achieved something which is approved by social arbiters.

Chapter Sixteen

The War on Genius

When we observe past societies, and how they were able to sustain geniuses and make us aware of the work of geniuses; the question arises: How was it that such simple and unselfconscious societies could spontaneously recognize and respond to something as complex and unpredictable and unique as a genius – when our much more prosperous and complex society cannot?

The reason is just that most human societies of the past, and certainly those societies where genius most thrived, were *serious*; they recognized that life is a serious business, that there is a reason for it all, a purpose to it all, and (in those societies where genius was most prevalent) that each person had a part to play – by contrast, at least in mainstream public discourse, modern Western society does not acknowledge any of this.

Charles Murray, in *Human Accomplishment*, suggested what we believe to be one correct answer: that for people in the past, the human condition was (in one way or another) eternally significant. Not only that, but life was perceived to be fragile, existential threats such as conquest or collapse were close at hand; and the people responsible for rulership knew a certain 'type' of personality had been able to solve major and unprecedented problems in the past.

But modern society has all-but lost this sense of the seriousness of life. We agree with Murray that this is substantially a consequence of the process of secularization, a matter of the loss of religion – since the most genius-conducive religions create a perspective extending beyond our mortal life and immediate sensory and emotional experiences. In public discourse, religion has been replaced by various secular, this-worldly socio-political ideologies. But all modern Western countries now share a triumphant, generically-Leftist ideology (*extremely* Leftist by world historical standards) that embraces all mainstream politics, administration, mass media and leadership. This underpins *all* the powerful political parties *including* those which are self-identified as Conservative, Republican, Nationalist, Libertarian and religious; and including leadership of all large organizations, institutions, and corporations – whatever their titles or self-definitions.

The modern ideology is compounded of human rights, equality, individuality, minimization of suffering and maximization of self-respect, diversity, inclusion and a strong emphasis on non-traditional sexual self-expression and identity. But the point is not so much these positive doctrines as the negative ones: this-life is all there is, and there is no meaning to life beyond the happiness or misery experienced; there is no objectivity to morality, humans are existentially alone and communication is uncertain and mostly a matter of self-deception. In sum, the modern ideology is secular and nihilistic, and modern people are short-termist, pleasure-orientated, and alienated.

One reason for the decline of religion is 'luxury' – that is the high levels of comfort and convenience in modern life, and the detachment from the natural world and immediate threats to survival. With the Industrial Revolution, the reduction of child and young adult mortality, the *de facto* elimination of starvation and mass lethal epidemics, the provision of near universal shelter and warmth etc.; plus actual and the expectation of continually-rising standards of living and ever-more-abundant provision of pleasures and entertainments – from all these factors and others the causes of our acute sufferings and fears have very much been taken away and, on a daily basis, we are so *insulated* that there seems to be no pressing need to believe that life has eternal significance.

Religiousness seems to be motivated and enforced by direct environmental stress. For instance, it reduces stress at the prospect of mortality by making us believe that our life is eternally significant. This is why perceived religious experiences tend to occur at times of danger or to people prone to stress.[107] Elimination of directly acting stresses tends to weaken or altogether abolish religion. In contrast, the abstract, free-floating, impossible-to-locate 'angst' of modern life clearly does not lead to religiousness; but rather to despair.

It seems paradoxical to moderns (who usually believe, or at least assert, that the existence of suffering refutes the reality of God); but the harder life is the more strongly religious people tend to be (for instance, the most recent significant Christian revival in Britain occurred during the Second World War); and the more comfortable and convenient life becomes, the less people seem to need religion, or to get immediate personal satisfaction from church membership and participation.

---

[107] See Dutton (2014), Op. cit. Also, Boyer, P. (2001). *Religion Explained: The Human Instincts that Fashion Gods, Spirits and Ancestors.* London: Heinemann; Inzlicht, M., I. McGregor, J. B. Hirsh & K. Nash. (2009). Neural markers of religious conviction. *Psychological Science*, 20: 385-392, Kay, A. C., Shepherd, S., Blatz, C. W. et al. (2010). For God (or) country: The hydraulic relation between government instability and belief in religious sources of control. *Journal of Personality and Social Psychology*, 99: 725-739; Lewis, G. & Bates, T. (2013). Common genetic influences underpin religiousness, community integration and existential uncertainty. *Journal of Research in Personality,* 47: 398-405. The way in which religion has been displaced and replaced by the mass media is the subject of Charlton, B.G. (2014) *Addicted to Distraction: Psychological Consequences of the Modern Mass Media*. Buckingham, UK: University of Buckingham Press.

Of course people still feel gnawing anxiety, depression and despair. But these do not trigger religiousness, being increasingly dealt with by 24/7 distraction provided by the mass media, interpersonal communication and quick transportation; any dysphoria (mild depression or otherwise unpleasant feelings) is dealt with by mass medication with tranquillizers and emotion-numbing 'antidepressants', 'antipsychotics' or 'mood stabilizers' (these words are placed in 'scare quotes' because they are all marketing terms with negligible scientific or clinical rationale).

Modern Man can, if he wishes, ignore his mortality, not think about it – so distant is it from everyday life; so many and so thick are the insulating layers between himself and the real environment of food, clothing, shelter and warmth; invaders, predators and parasites. He can live absorbed in a world of drugged distraction. And this is, pretty much, the totality of the modern vision of life.

As such, the Endogenous personality, or potential genius, is perceived as a problem for modernity because the genius is only appreciated, only makes people happy, when there is an acknowledged crisis. And when there is no obvious crisis or, if there is, it is so far in the future that most of us lack the future-orientation (in other words, the intelligence) to worry about it or even believe in it;

or when we can simply be persuaded (by the mass media) to deny or ignore the crisis, or re-label crisis as progress . . . then the genius becomes just an annoying and apparently unproductive person: a social irritant rather than a potential societal saviour.

So, modern society is in practice indifferent or hostile to genius and the products of genius; since we are complacent, trivial and evasive. For us, problems are merely part of the world of sensation and entertainment – continually defined then re-defined; and genius is just one of many millions of things to be taken-up, contemplated briefly, then impatiently set aside in the unending quest for novel stimulations.

Also, modern institutions are almost always controlled by managers; and managers do not participate directly with the primary function of organizations (e.g. managers of research do not do research, managers of hospitals do not provide health care, managers of widget factories do not carve the widgets) – therefore for the manager (*qua* manager) 'the bottom line', the effective 'reality' is ultimately the perception of others. This is why, as management takeover has become more complete in The West; management of perceptions, impressions, opinions etc. has come to dominate organizations. For management, 'truth' is what people currently think is true, and if what-people-think can be shaped to suit expediency– then so can 'truth'.

Therefore, it seems that modern society is indifferent/ hostile to genius for the simple reason that as – a human group – *we perceive no real and urgent sense of group self-interest*. We cannot really believe in real-problems and the real-need for real-solutions – we deny that there is a price to pay for survival, and that genius is one of these prices.

And insofar as modern society is aware of geniuses having provided solutions to real and vital societal problems, these answers are typically vehemently rejected. We don't acknowledge tough problems demanding tough solutions – we instead demand easy answers. Indeed, we really don't want answers – because we pretend things are already solved, or that solutions just happen, naturally, as part of the nature of things; or that what we currently happen-to want-to do will also (miraculously!) provide exactly the answers we most need.

This is significant because we believe genius to be group selected. Modern man seemingly cannot any longer believe that human group cohesion is vital for continued existence and prospering – we see ourselves as in essence atomistic, autonomous individuals and not as integral members of a group. All this can be seen in the often-remarked loss of social cohesion at the level of workplaces, neighbourhoods, clubs, hobbies, churches, schools, colleges, crafts and professions – what is termed the decline in Civil Society – all these groups have been weakened, subverted or even destroyed by The State to which most people now look to provide their wants. Since civic involvement has been shown to be positively associated with intelligence, we should not be surprised to observe its decline.[108]

As already discussed, it is not just intelligence which is declining but also other adaptations such as the General Factor of Personality: so we are on average less pro-social, more anti-social and asocial. And fertility is inversely associated with education, as well as with intelligence – expanding education to include ever wider sectors of the population for ever longer periods of life has therefore (independently) imposed further damage on the fertility of the most intelligent on top of long term intelligence related trends.[109] Educational success is predicted by the GFP. So, we are becoming less Agreeable, less Conscientious, less group-oriented in multiple ways. Indeed, mutation accumulation would be expected to damage all types of evolved adaptation; perhaps first and especially social adaptations, which tend to be most

[108] Deary, I., Batty, G. D. & Gales, C. (2008). Childhood intelligence predicts voter turnout, voter preferences and political involvement in adulthood; the 1970 cohort. *Intelligence,* 36: 548-555.
[109] Herrnstein, R. & Murray, C. (1994). *The Bell Curve: Intelligence and Class Structure in American Life*. New York: Free Press.

sensitive to brain pathologies (psychiatric and neurological diseases show-up in social deficits and pathologies more sensitively than in other aspects of functionality).

In sum, under modern conditions individual selection subverts group selection, individual selfishness subverts group selfishness – and each person increasingly aspires to be a 'free rider': getting more than he gives, living at the expense of the group as chronically unemployed, chronically 'sick', long-term retired; living life as a continual party, travelogue or holiday.

Short-term selfishness replaces long-term groupishness – and an utterly ineffectual, feel-good emotion of universal or 'global' benevolence has replaced the tough choices, personal involvement, hard work and specific duties imposed by long-term loyalty to defined groups.

The problem of evil geniuses

Although we argue for the importance of creativity in human affairs, and therefore of the importance of the creatives who do the primary work of creativity, it should not be forgotten that creativity is not only a positive human value in itself, but is also a means to an end; and that end may be socially good or bad, creative and cohesive, or socially subversive and destructive. As society has lost a sense of its eternal significance, creative types – indeed geniuses – can be found in the pursuit of things that a 'traditional society' would regard as 'evil.'

Modern society has indeed become more and more 'evil' – which is to say (providing here a brief definition of evil) organized in pursuit of destruction of The Good in the traditional sense of the word – the Good being (roughly) the transcendental values of Truth, Beauty and Virtue, underpinned by a sense of unity and the eternal.

Thus modern leadership in many areas of life is engaged, both passively by neglect and actively by policy, in destruction of truth, beauty and virtue – indeed, frequently in *inversion* of values; so that modern ideas of TB&V are often the opposite of traditional: for instance, 'subversive' is now a term of praise. That is to say, modern leadership embodies and enforces a morality which takes reality and turns it upside-down – so that good becomes evil and vice versa. This Nietzschean project of 'the transvaluation of all values' is far advanced, albeit incompletely realized, and indeed it cannot ever be fully realized – nonetheless, 'progress' towards its realization continues incrementally and cumulatively. In such a context, it is unsurprising that most existent creativity is harnessed in pursuit of this 'evil'. After all, genius is a form of power, and in an evil world power is likely to be used for evil purposes.

In the first place, much of this distinctively modern form of evil by inversion is a product of highly creative persons, such as Nietzsche himself, and lesser emulators who not only extrapolated his ideas, but creatively enhanced them. Examples include many of the modernist artistic subversives of early 20th century art. We have already mentioned Picasso, Schoenburg and James Joyce – who seem to have inflicted net harm; and there are many equally influential partial-geniuses such as Duchamp, John Cage, Ezra Pound, William Burroughs, and Samuel Beckett – men whose considerable creative gifts were harnessed to what was sometimes actively *intended* to be, and sometimes merely *turned-out* to be, subversive, inversional and destructive agendas.

In essence, and in opposition to the past 'cohesion geniuses' of religion, philosophy, literature, music, and art that we mentioned earlier; modern 'evil geniuses' have used their creativity to undermine rather than strengthen social cohesion; to argue or demonstrate that there is no such thing as truth, or that the false is true; to assert that life has no meaning, to assert that forms of immorality should be praised as virtuous, and to reject beauty in favour of originality or even to try to promote ugliness as beauty.

In other words, they used their genius to reverse the values of the past and promote a dark, nihilistic and despairing Void of a life.

Secondly, due to the fact of creativity being part of the personality type of 'Psychoticism' – creatives may tend to be more-than-usually vulnerable to the consequences of impulsivity and less restrained by social ethics: they are lone wolves with a potentially predatory attitude which is relatively easily corrupted by short-term and selfish incentives, as we have seen of Jung.

Most often this can be seen in sexual and monetary exploitativeness, shirking, lying, cheating, seducing and sponging of the stereotypical 'Bohemian' lifestyle; that once defined became widely emulated (for instance by the Beats of the 1950s, or the Hippies of the sixties) – with predictably self-destructive effect; for instance in the lifestyles, anti-morality and premature deaths of writers such as Arthur Rimbaud (1854-1891),[110] Oscar Wilde (1854-1900)[111], Jack Kerouac (1922-1969) and the numerous talented casualties of the rock and pop music scene.[112]

---

[110] White, E. (2008). *Rimbaud: The Double Life of a Rebel*. London: Grove.

[111] Ellmann, R. (1988). *Oscar Wilde*. New York: Vintage Books.

[112] Hunt, T. (1981). *Kerouac's Crooked Road*. Hamden: Archon Books.

Thirdly, creatives – who might in principle exercise their creativity on anything – will find, but may not notice, that they have themselves been pointed-at traditional institutions and values; in a context where creativity is akin to subversion, where successful destruction of approved targets is applauded, and accorded high status and material support. For instance, in the post-1945 era and increasingly, positive depictions of extramarital or unconventional sex, drug-taking and criminality were given publicity and elite status; while mockery or subversion of Christian, 'Bourgeois' or Middle Class values was similarly applauded.

In sum, modern creatives are highly likely to be amateur or professional, intentional or accidental destroyers of the Good – in their net effect if not wholly. This is one of the horrors of our uniquely nihilistic world.

Humans have always failed to attain The Good due to our own weaknesses and bad motivation – but we are now in the situation where it is normal (also legally and officially encouraged and rewarded) actively to attack The Good, by many means and on many fronts – so that both creative ability and hard-working conscientiousness do not merely fail to reach their promise and their ideals – but are harnessed to work against The Good.

In sum, most modern creatives inflict either more, or less, harmful outcomes overall; and the more effective their creativity, the greater the harm they inflict.

Chapter Fifteen

What to do?

Throughout this book, we seem to have evolved such a distinctive perspective on the nature and effect of Genius, and proposed so many new and unfamiliar ideas, that we can hardly suppose that anyone else would be likely to hold exactly identical views. Most people will therefore need to regard this book as a set of stimuli for further thought and appraisal (or, a collection of what Marshall McLuhan used to call 'probes').

In the end we harbour some ambivalence about the place of genius in the modern world. In a rotten and corrupt society, genius is probably more likely to lead to harm than good, for the same reason that any machine will usually do more harm than good when put into the hands of a wicked or stupid person.

But on the other hand, the work of genius is the only realistic hope of Western Man escaping a catastrophic outcome in a society far advanced on the road to ruin; because only the genius can make the qualitative creative leap to discover paths and options invisible to the normal man.

This may be a matter of creating new methods, but perhaps what modern Man most needs is not better means to an end; but a restored sense of the meaning, purpose, reality and community of life. What we lack most of all is motivation – and if a modern genius, or group of geniuses, could somehow create a new basis for motivation – then this would perhaps do more than anything else to improve the prospects of a better future.

1. The modern world has been necessarily based on the work of a concentration of European geniuses from the Middle Ages and into the middle twentieth century; but genius has been disappearing rapidly over the past century, and appears to be extinct in several domains. There exists a state of Genius Famine.

2. This situation has been partly caused, and partly exacerbated by the (seemingly irrational, but sociologically explicable) fact that the modern world has become (and is becoming more) hostile to the Endogenous personality who is the potential basis for genius, and even to the work of actual geniuses; so that the relatively few geniuses who emerge are nowadays usually kept from having any chance of significant influence.

3. On the one hand there is a 'famine' of genius – which afflicts science, technology, the arts, politics, philosophy, law... pretty much everything; with very few people of even potential or partial genius now working within these fields. Yet, on

the other hand, within these fields, among professionals and experts, there is near-zero awareness, and indeed vehement denial of the blatantly obvious, rapid, and near total decline in genius.

4. Obscuration of the true state of things has been achieved by two opposite (and contradictory) strategies – denying that there is such a thing as real genius, and re-labelling non-creative fake, novelty-cobblers as real geniuses – using mechanisms such as awarding them 'genius' prizes or by redefining merely fashionable novelties as examples of genuine creative excellence.

5. Modern people are of considerably lower average and peak 'general intelligence' than in the past – so such geniuses as emerge will generally be figures of lesser scope and creative impact than in the past. And insofar as the generation upon generation decline of genius is due to an accumulation of deleterious genetic mutations (caused by the relaxation of natural selection, especially via child mortality) then this would also be expected to damage the evolved and adaptive personality complex of the Endogenous personality.

6. So future geniuses will be lesser figures than in the past: less able, less inner-directed and inner-motivated, with less effective inner-evaluations, and demonstrating less independence and commitment in their creativity.

7. However, even a 'local genius', a minor figure by world-historical standards, still provides the *possibility* of a genuinely creative answer to real problems. No geniuses – no such possibilities.

So, what can we do about all this? How can we improve the situation with respect to geniuses?

Probably there is not much we can do as individuals – indeed, probably the problem of the decline of genius cannot be *solved*, even if there were awareness and understanding of the problem and the determined will to solve it: which there is not.

The only solutions that have been seriously proposed would, in our view, simply not work. Sir Francis Galton (1822-1911) highlighted the problem of the less intelligent outbreeding the more intelligent in Victorian England in his 1869 book *Hereditary Genius*.[113] Later, he argued that this could be solved by a programme of eugenics which

---

[113] Galton, F. (1869). *Hereditary Genius: An Inquiry into its Laws and Consequences*. London: MacMillan.

would financially incentivise the more intelligent to have the most children combined with inculcating people with a kind of latter-day religiosity which emphasized the importance of improving the 'human stock.'[114] Others, such as Richard Lynn in his book *Eugenics: A Reassessment*[115] have defended Galton but provided more detail, for example advocating licensing to have children with the permitted number dictated by the couple's intelligence level.

However, even leaving aside religious prohibitions; it seems to us that there are a number of serious practical problems with these views. Limiting the fertility of the majority of the population in this way could only be achieved in a stringent dictatorship based around, as Galton suggested, some form of 'secular religion' of eugenics. This would entail a society of conformity and coercion, which could potentially be highly problematic for generating new ideas or correcting wrong ideas. It is quite possible that such policies would result in protest, rebellion and war, potentially worsening living conditions. Indeed, the toughest problem, and the greatest controversy, would probably come from trying to make the

---

[114] Galton, F. (1904). Eugenics: Its Definition, Scope and Aims. *The American Journal of Sociology,* 10: 1-25.
[115] Lynn, R. (2001). *Eugenics: A Reassessment.* Westport: Praeger.

modern secular elites have (on average) above-replacement numbers of children, since all over the world the fertility of those of highest intelligence and most education has fallen very low as soon as contraception has become available.

Moreover, as we have shown, dysgenics on intelligence is caused not just by dysgenic breeding but also, and probably mainly, by mutation accumulation. Accordingly, the only way, if we follow Galton, to reverse dysgenics would be (at minimum) the monstrous policy of allowing to die, to sterilize, or (most effectively) inflict death upon, about half of the children born in each generation.

In other words, effective eugenics would entail Man artificially restoring the pre-modern harshness of natural selection; and thereby reversing what could regarded the single greatest triumph of the Industrial Revolution (which, arguably, has been the near elimination from modern human experience of what used to be the almost universal tragedy of parents suffering the premature death of several or most of their children).

So in practice we would not be likely to do more than merely somewhat ameliorate the genius famine.

On the whole it seems that we should simply do our best to find, support and take notice of genius: to make the most of what genius yet remains.

The hope is that geniuses, by the fact of their genuine creativity, would be our best, and perhaps our *only*, chance of finding an escape route from a trajectory which – by conventional analysis – appears certainly to be terminal for Western civilization.

Chapter Sixteen

In Search of the Boy Genius

If there was a sense of real crisis, and urgent sense of need, there might emerge a better and more wide-spread 'search process' for discovering geniuses: a more effective way of unearthing more individuals from the declining pool of potential geniuses and giving them a better chance of coming-through to a position where they might attain the best work of which they were capable – and then taking some notice of it.

Our description of the Endogenous personality throughout this book would, we hope, make possible and effective this search process: for perhaps the first time, people in search of potential geniuses would know what it was they were looking for – the combination of inner motivation and intuitive thinking with high intelligence.

They would also know what they were *not* looking for: the empathic, sociable, conscientious, popular and balanced 'Head Girl' type, who, despite his or her many virtues and general valuableness – is the opposite of a genius.

Yet, even to write that paragraph is to see that it will likely not happen, and also perhaps why it will not happen. How could a society which is root-and-branch hostile to exactly the kind of person who might (but perhaps won't) eventually become a genius then make a breakthrough of genius impact, do anything effective to find, nurture and support geniuses? Our society typically sees the actually-existing genius as a problem to be eliminated, rather than the best, and perhaps only, only hope of civilizational salvation.

And there is the paradox of organizing society to encourage the emergence of the disorganized and disorganizing and disruptive. But if something of the sort was actually put into effect (and this might well be a plot for a science fiction novel, perhaps by Philip K Dick), then it could happen by means of a program of psychological profiling and deep aptitude testing by 'genius masters' rather like the process which already exists for discovering talent in musical performance – the ways of discovering a great concert pianist or an operatic soloist, or chess grandmasters. That is, a multitude of individual coaches, teachers and Maestros would seek-out and take-on promising youngsters for training; and there would be a variety of exhibitions and competitions aimed at evaluating both achieved performance and (more important) potential.

The Endogenous personality is, in fact, usually detectable from around school age; in his three aspects of high intelligence, intuitive thinking and inner motivation. Intelligence can be tested, with fair reliability and validity; intuitive thinking may be discerned by sympathetic observation of dreaminess and inspired insights; inner motivation will emerge in eccentric and individualistic patterns of interests and behaviours. Armed with this knowledge it is, in principle, quite possible to pick-out the Boy Genius type (including a minority of girls) and help to smooth his path, and recognize his distinctive needs and vulnerabilities.

The framework is that talent-with-potential (typically, high technical ability in a context of the Endogenous personality) is being discovered then developed to a point where the talent can take-over its own development. The apprentice would need to find, and trust, a Master (who would himself need to be an Endogenous personality). The Master would need to want to find, and work with, the best apprentices. And the Masters would be in control of the system (*not* Head Girls or bureaucrats or committees). Because only the Masters can perceive what is going-on – can perceive the difference between mere high ability and the potential for creative genius. But aside from that, there is no 'system'. No formal requirements. No standard progression. No accreditation of any significance.

But it is equally, perhaps more, essential that the potential genius be given the kind of personal and emotional support he needs – or at least that he be not assaulted by what he would perceive as additional stresses. Many (not all) geniuses are (as

Ruskin perceived, and knew from personal experience) unusually childlike and dependent; and benefit from a higher level and greater duration of 'looking after' – which would typically come from the family, but if not them then someone else trustworthy, caring, and with the genius's best interests at heart. The sad experience of William Sidis – thrown by his parents, still a child-like child, into the rough turmoil of Harvard – should be a warning in this regard.

The above may sound all too privileged for the already-privileged, terribly elitist, very esoteric. It is a statement of the need for special treatment for special people. And it sees talent and the potential for genius as essentially innate. If you haven't got it you can't do it; and if even you have, you probably won't. It asks for everything that modern culture despises, and indeed regards as immoral.

Furthermore, this is anti-democratic, anti-popular, and aristocratic. High intellectual ability is itself very rare, but high ability in the context of an Endogenous personality is rarer still. The process of finding Boy Geniuses is about searching for a very few diamonds among great heaps of (useful) coal – but with a distracting and deceptive proportion of gaudy 'costume jewellery' (pretend diamonds, pseudo-geniuses) taking the form of un-creative skill and fake creativity.

In conclusion, if modern society was concerned with its own continuation – which very clearly it is not, being instead self-loathing and covertly devoted to its own extinction – then something of this kind would need to occur to locate and empower sufficient numbers of geniuses to maintain the frequent and relevant breakthroughs necessary to enable continued growth in efficiency and capability.

But, overall, it seems that we have to accept that Western civilization will decline. It is, essentially, inevitable. Life will go backwards, life will become simpler, harsher – much less comfortable, much more serious.

Eventually, and after considerable suffering; like it or not; perhaps enough people will come to feel part of groups, to see the benefits of genius to the group, and to recognize the necessity of genius.

And the genius will again resume his proper role in society.

Conclusion: Seven statements about genius

1. We need to recognize that support for genius is social self-interest – it is a risky investment, true; but when it pays off, a genius yields vastly more benefit than he costs.

2. The benefits yielded by genius are not obtainable in any other way.

3. Genius is born and not made. Training of non-geniuses will not yield more geniuses.

4. Genius can be identified, and may be encouraged and flourish; or alternatively genius can be ignored, thwarted, suppressed – and rendered irrelevant.

5. A genius is a difficult, eccentric, asocial person who – despite this – exists in order to promote the good of the group.

6. Yet, although strong in self-motivation, self-determination and autonomy – a genius is normally a sensitive and emotionally vulnerable person. He can be dismayed, demoralized, cor-

rupted or driven to despair – and his potential will then be diminished or destroyed.

7. In future most genius will be 'local' (by our current standards), rather than international: a shaman rather than an Einstein. This is the best that can realistically be hoped-for – but a local genius is better than no genius at all.

About the Authors

Edward Dutton is Adjunct Professor of the Anthropology of Religion at Oulu University in Finland and an independent scholar. He read Theology at Durham University and researched a PhD in Religious Studies at Aberdeen University, focusing on anthropology. This was published as *Meeting Jesus at University* (Ashgate, 2008). Among his other books are a study of Finnish culture, *The Finnuit* (Akademiai Kiado, 2009), *Culture Shock and Multiculturalism* (Cambridge Scholars, 2012) and *Religion and Intelligence* (Ulster Institute for Social Research, 2014). His most recent book (with Richard Lynn) is *Race and Sport* (Ulster Institute for Social Research, 2015). His research has been reported in, and he has also written for, various national newspapers and magazines. He can be found online at www.edwarddutton.wordpress.com

Bruce G Charlton is Visiting Professor of Theoretical Medicine at the University of Buckingham and Reader in Evolutionary Psychiatry at Newcastle University. Bruce has an unusually broad intellectual experience: he graduated with honours from the Newcastle Medical School, took a doctorate at the Medical Research Council

Neuroendocrinology group, and did postgraduate training in psychiatry and public health. He has held university lectureships in physiology, anatomy, epidemiology, and psychology; and has a Masters degree in English Literature from Durham. From 2003-10 Bruce solo-edited Medical Hypotheses; a monthly international journal that published frequently speculative, sometimes amusing, and often controversial ideas and theories across the whole of medicine and beyond. He has published considerably more than two hundred scientific papers and academic essays in these fields, and contributed journalism to UK national broadsheets and weekly magazines. Bruce is author of *Thought Prison: The Fundamental Nature of Political Correctness* (2011); *Not Even Trying: The Corruption of Real Science* (2012) and *Addicted to Distraction: Psychological Consequences of the Modern Mass Media* (2014) all published by University of Buckingham Press. *Intelligence, Personality and Genius* is Bruce's blog, where many of the ideas for this book were developed: iqpersonalitygenius.blogspot.co.uk